About the Cover

This is an old handmade rocking chair with strips of bark carefully woven into a pattern for the back and seat. It is a plain, earthy and creative piece of work by a grandfather in Breathitt County, Kentucky who was teaching his grandson the trade. My father special ordered this chair and deemed it important that I meet this craftsman and his grandson. This chair, which I inherited, sits on the porch of a restored cabin near Renfro Valley, Kentucky.

Cover design by Keith Gilberson

For our mail carrier who has made getting a mail a pleasure. Wishing you the best in your new position. Thank you! The Frazier's Tom + Joy

Come Sit a Spell

Memoirs of an Appalachian Son

By Thomas D. Frazier

INFINITY
PUBLISHING

ISBN 978-0-7414-5782-0

Printed in the United States of America

Published October 2019

INFINITY PUBLISHING
1094 New DeHaven Street, Suite 100
West Conshohocken, PA 19428-2713
Toll-free (877) BUY BOOK
Local Phone (610) 941-9999
Fax (610) 941-9959
Info@buybooksontheweb.com
www.buybooksontheweb.com

Contents

Dedicated to Joy for the love, support and encouragement she has shown to me over the past fifty years.

Foreword

Many of us, when we reach retirement age and beyond, tend to reassure ourselves that we have done some good in the world and perhaps might have some useful advice to others. The increasing number of published memories testifies to this need. We reflect on our careers, origins, our people whoever they might be, and what we learned from them. We think of our parents and grandparents, other kin and neighbors, and especially teachers, or preachers, or friends who have contributed to our lives – to our outlook, way of thinking, core beliefs, philosophy of life, and how we see the human condition. Rev. Tom Frazier reflects here on his greatest influence. A Presbyterian minister, he thinks first not of John Knox, or other learned and persuasive teachers from his seminary days, but of his quiet and humble father Millard "Frank" Frazier who came from a late-formed Kentucky County along the Big Sandy River that divides the state from West Virginia.

His father was not the only person close to him who was from Lawrence County. In his wanderings, Tom met and married Joy Adams, a registered nurse and solo singer, who just happened to be from the same county. Four other notable people were also native to this county. Fred Vinson was born near Louisa, Kentucky in 1890. He went on to serve as a U.S. Representative, U.S Secretary of Treasury, and thirteenth chief justice of the United States. Cratis D. Williams (1911-1985) descended from the last legal distillers of whiskey on Caines Creek. At sixteen, he published an essay, "Why a Mountain Boy Should be Proud." He went on to become a scholar of Appalachia, a linguist, and professor of English, dean of the graduate school, and acting chancellor of Appalachian State University and his dissertation on Appalachian Literature was a three-volume work of 1650 pages. He was known as the "Father of Appalachia Studies." Paul E. Patton was born in Fallsburg in 1937. He graduated in engineering from the University of Kentucky, became a coal operator for 20 years, making himself a fortune. He then entered politics, serving as Pike County, Kentucky, judge-executive from 1982-1991, was elected governor of Kentucky in 1995 and served two terms. In 2009, he became president of Pikeville College. Ricky Skaggs was born at Cordelle, Kentucky, in 1954. His father Hobart Skaggs taught him to play various musical instruments, and he was so precocious, he played on stage with Bill Monroe at age 5 and on television with Lester Flatt and Earl Scruggs at 7. His professional career began at 16 with Ralph Stanley and his Clinch Mountain Boys bluegrass band. He has headed his own country and bluegrass bands, played also in Emmy Lou Harris's band, is a member of the *Grand Ole Opry,* and has won a total of 14 Grammies.

One might say that the gene pool of Lawrence County is as strong as anyplace else.

Tom Frazier was born in Charleston, West Virginia. His father had sought work in Florida, and Tom's early years were happy ones in Orlando. He was devastated at age 14 when the family moved back to Appalachia, to the industrial town of Ashland, Kentucky. He found himself a stranger in a strange land. It took him years to understand the values that influenced his father's move back to the mountains. In Orlando, he remembered that his father's innate sense of person relatedness made him pause to talk with all sort of people – at the gas station, the store, or on the street, and to find out what he could about the lives they had led. To him personhood was the highest value. He noted that air conditioning and television had trapped people inside their houses and damaged this sense of relatedness and of community. Front porches were becoming obsolete. The title of this book suggests a profound lesson in how people and communities have changed from the time when we had the leisure for 'front-porch sitting', with kin and neighbors and strangers as well.

While they were living in Florida, on Sunday morning, probably on Saturday evening as well, the 'Renfro Valley Barn Dance' brought music right into their home. His father was happy when he could sing along with these radio voices, but reflected unbounded joy when he took the family to see the cast of the shows in a personal appearance in Orlando. The lyrics and tunes reinforced the values that he had been taught in Lawrence County – having to do with faith, relationships, family, sense of place, and community, all wrapped in a nostalgic package.

Tom Frazier has taken his father's invitation to "Come Sit a Spell" as a metaphor for a way of life that allowed us time to sit and visit and reflect, as compared to the frantic activity that is common in much of modern life. Frazier graduated from the Louisville Presbyterian Theological Seminary and invested his ministerial career primarily in pastoral counseling. Thus, the personal has always been topmost in his concern for a way to seek better relationships with one another and with the Creator. He has read widely in relation to his primary purpose, and has clarified his intent and purpose in his poetry and prose, thus offering suggestions for attaining a wider and more rewarding temporal and spiritual life.

Loyal Jones

Preface

I would like to say that I have always been spellbound by my father but it's just not so, at least not until I became more mature in my faith. By faith I mean not just in God but also in myself and in the appreciation of my creation in which my father was so instrumental. I find it most difficult to separate God from my experiences in life and especially my life as I have come to see it from the inspiration of my father. Growing up in my father's house I never thought I would say such a thing – strange how time changes our perspective of people and situations. Yet over time I have been unable to separate my father's influence from Appalachia where he was born and lived until a young man. Nor did I ever imagine marrying a woman from the same county in Eastern Kentucky. As a boy I heard many a story about Lawrence County, which seemed so distant and of little concern to me, and yet I always felt Dad's passion in his voice and in his eyes, as tears formed when he so fondly told of his early years in this wonderful part of the world.

As I began writing I found it was impossible to write about how Appalachia has formed and shaped me, apart from telling stories about my father. Not only stories about him but all stories, since everything I have experienced has been filtered through his influence. The way I hear things or see things is somehow a gift, which I have received from the man that not only fathered me but also spiritually shaped me in some mysterious manner. This book is an attempt to put this in writing, which I have found impossible apart from stories and poetry. The poetry is most important in that it would come to me when all else was mute. To me the poetry is deeply spiritual – words from God when all else failed. In fact I have often thought that my book should be a book of annotated poetry and yet, in a manner, maybe that is just what I have put together.

Dad taught me the meaning of Psalm 46:10 without ever having to read it to me or point it out as being important. *"Be still, and know that I am God!"* was a way of life for my Dad. He had the greatest appreciation of all people and was always eager to listen and, in reverence, find all moments to be spiritual moments. I have thought this to be my inspiration for going into a counseling ministry. I have found it not only easy to listen with interest but find, in listening, a spiritual depth. To sit a spell in the Appalachian spirit is to appreciate life, to listen and learn from others, to seek silence and so much more as we learn to *"Be still, and know that I am God!"*

In this time of hard work, materialism and intellectualism, the invitation to "come sit a spell" appears to be of little value to the "left brain' individuals who saturate our culture. The invitation to 'come sit a spell' is a deeply spiritual calling to those who can recognize it as so and engage in dialogue, which can confirm who we are and whose we are in an extremely busy and narcissistic society. I remain appreciative to my wife, Joy, who has supported and encouraged me in the writing of this book, and for the help and encouragement I have received from my good friend Loyal Jones. But most of all I remain especially thankful for my father without whom there would be no book.

Thomas Frazier

GENESIS

Roads run backward
as well as forward,
dreams and memories merge,
reflection and anticipation,
created or creating
beginnings or endings,
life runs shallow without both –
Genesis and Exodus we embrace.

Reaching back to reach forward
finding faith to live by
and hope to thrive.
Reflections can make us cry
while visions elate us
or might reversal apply?
Life can be most ominous –
volumes filled without ending.

The body and its senses provide a primary and life long sense of identity. Through them we gain early awareness of others and ourselves. When we can open to experience their subtle messages, we come to realize that, like a good mother, the body itself has held us, constantly present through sickness and health, through shame and ecstasy, alone and in relationship with others. It accompanies us throughout life.

Sylvia Brinton Perera

BEGINNINGS

Life is difficult when you are thirteen years old and your parents up and move to what seems like another world. In fact, Kentucky was and is an entirely different world from Orlando, Florida, especially back before Cape Canaveral and Disney World. I had lots of friends and was well established in school. The neighborhood was my life and I knew it like the back of my hand. My best friends grew up with me and lived in this same neighborhood. This was where we rode bikes, built forts, made slingshots and shot birds and squirrels with BB guns and had our secret hiding places. It was in this neighborhood that Gordon, a beautiful Irish setter, befriended all of us as he ran with us and swam in the lakes with us and even ate with us. How could I do without Gordon? I had even shared my ice cream with Gordon! Gordon had the reputation of stealing chickens out of a neighbor's lot and when we found Gordon with a dead chicken we would take it from him and bury it. This was our way of protecting Gordon, for we knew how angry the chicken's owner would become and try to get rid of Gordon. Funny thing is, none of us knew who really owned Gordon. I guess it didn't matter because he just seemed like a communal pet and best friend and who owned him didn't really matter; in fact it would be a bit troubling to think Gordon was owned by anyone.

As I reflect on Gordon I realize he has become an icon, a window by which I remember all that was once important to me, all that was taken away in a most significant moment of my life. Gordon is my childhood, my innocence, and my beginning, that place which had roots that nurtured my soul. Gordon was strength, beauty and my friend who loved me unconditionally. When I left for uncharted territory Gordon grieved with me mostly because he understood that most of my resources were being left behind.

I now realize just how depressed I really was when my family moved from Orlando. I had no skills or abilities to function as a healthy thirteen year old in a foreign land. I felt just like the Hebrew people in exile when their captors, the Assyrians, requested that they sing some of their beautiful ballads. The Hebrew people responded saying, "How could we sing the Lord's song in a foreign land? (Psalm 137:4)? It appears to me that depression is a lot like not being at home, or forced to live in a foreign land. It is even more depressing when those in that land are expecting a good performance. No wonder I missed Gordon so much and could only light a candle at his holy icon.

The suburbs of Orlando were an ideal place for children to grow, with little or no crime, beautiful weather year around except for a few days in the winter, and clear blue lakes that dotted the entire area. Orange groves were in abundance where, as a young boy, I played in secret with my friends. Parents would have been horrified to find us throwing hard green oranges at one another that would leave welts and bruises. But even more horrifying was the time a friend took a box of twelve-gauge shotgun shells from his father's hunting stock and met us deep within the orange grove under a large grapefruit tree loaded with fruit. We built a fire under that grapefruit tree and carefully placed each shotgun shell upright within the wood that was stacked for a fire. It was agreed that while my friends took their positions behind trees that would guard them from the explosion, I would light the fire and run like hell! I had chosen a tree to hide behind. With both fear and excitement, the fire was lit and I ran behind my chosen tree. It took longer than any of us imagined for the fire to get hot enough to set off the shells. It seemed like an eternity, but when they went off it was something to behold! It was better than any fireworks I have ever attended, mainly because of the anticipation and satisfaction of doing such a thing. When it was over we came out from our hiding places to find ourselves standing in the rain of grapefruit juice. What an experience! We were amazed and excited that we were able to accomplish such a phenomenon. My friends and I then ran through the grove to the lake's edge where we had found a drainage line running to the street. It was a long crawl through this drainage line but when we got to the street there was room for three of us to sit at eye level with pavement as we peered through the drain that had been cut in the cement curbing. Here we smoked cigarettes that had been taken from the same source as the shotgun shells. We would retell the event back in the orange grove, laughing and coughing with watery eyes from the cigarette smoke.

Leaving Orlando was about the worst thing that ever happened to me and I was not going to get over it quickly or easily. We lived in a most modest house, but it was home, a home that was deeply rooted and grounded in the neighborhood. In the 40's before T.V. and air conditioning doors and windows were always open and everyone knew everyone's business. There were no secrets and right in the middle of a conversation or argument there might stand one of the neighbors who just walked in from next door. We lived next door to a family that consisted of two young girls and as they grew up we heard all the joys and sadness that transpired along their journey toward maturity. People sat on either the front porch or the back porch and neighbors were not only welcomed, but also expected to drop in for a spell. It would be years later when I heard my father say, "No one needs anyone anymore," as he walked about the neighborhood looking for someone to talk with. My Dad would go on to say that central air and heating and T.V. had caused people to stay indoors with the drapes closed enjoying their own climate and being entertained by the T.V. This has become even truer with our advanced technology, or is it really advanced if it keeps us from experiencing our neighborhood?

Many years later when my office received a computer with the Internet and e-mail, my secretary said, "I guess we don't even have to talk with one another now." What would my father think now with all the technology? He would most likely be highly disturbed, if not angry, that people don't have more time to relate to one another. Perhaps relate is the wrong word. I think what Dad would miss is the opportunity to converse or experience a type of personal, social and spiritual intercourse that is not possible by e-mail. The concept of neighbor or community appears to be central to the Gospel, right up there with peace and perhaps the two cannot be separated no matter how hard we try. When Jesus was asked what the greatest commandment was he said, "You shall love the Lord your God with all your heart, and with all your soul, and with all your mind. This is the greatest and first commandment. The second is like it: You shall love your neighbor as yourself" (Matthew 22:37-39). Can neighborliness, community or peace be equivalent with love of God and love of self? To have neighborliness, community or peace, is not leisure necessary – the spiritual capacity for freedom – the ability to make room or space for one's neighbor? This means to be able to do nothing that something might take place in our lives – a paradox that must not only be understood but also appreciated and incorporated into our lives. This is a difficult concept or paradox for the modern person to value in that we still carry much of our Puritan tradition around with us which says that doing nothing is idleness, wastefulness and even sinful. Therefore the front porch sits empty while we busy ourselves and become increasingly distant from neighbor, God and ourselves, and increasingly with the potential for stress, rage and violence.

One of my fondest memories was going to get gasoline with Dad at the neighborhood filling station. This was before self-service when the checking of the oil level, tire pressure and washing the windshield was routine. Dad would ask many questions, such as "How long have you been working here?" and "Do you have a family?" This was only the beginning. My Dad probably enjoyed people more than anyone I have ever known. He just couldn't get enough of them. Getting gas was not just a quick and easy exercise, rather an adventure that might end up taking thirty to forty minutes which is a long time to a nine-year-old boy. When I would complain Dad would point out all that I was missing by not paying attention and would often say, "Listen to this man, he has been around and seen many things." On and on he would go, "This man has worked here for 20 years, just think about that!" Dad would always leave such a conversation a better man, and thankful for the experience, and the other person would always feel so much better about themselves as a result of not only Dad's listening ability but the affirmation that he gave freely and genuinely. Dad's message seemed always to be one of gratitude for other people, which he never forgot. When we left this service station I just knew that this was not the end of this experience but that I would hear about it repeatedly in some context, either at the dinner table or his retelling of this man's life to the next-door neighbor. I know that Dad was grateful for his life but to hear him tell it his life was nothing compared to the everyday people with which he came in contact.

Sunday mornings my father became most animated by listening to the Renfro Valley radio program that was broadcast from Rockcastle County, Kentucky. It was through this program that Dad could stay in touch with his roots while listening to traditional music and various stories from the hill country of his homeland. Dad would go through the house clapping his hands and singing along with the radio. There was one particular character that Dad enjoyed by the name of 'Granny'. As I remember 'Granny' Harper epitomized Appalachia through her music, stories and humor. Dad approached me one day saying, "Tom, I just heard that Renfro Valley is coming to the Coliseum here in Orlando. You and I must go."

I will never forget this experience. I don't think I have ever seen Dad so excited. The anticipation built over the days until this great event when my father and I attended, not just a performance, but rather a cultural event equivalent only to a family reunion. During the intermission Dad diligently sought out 'Granny' and unapologetically approached her saying. 'Granny', where in Kentucky are you from?" In response 'Granny' said, "Jessamine County, Nicholasville, hoss country", and quickly skittered off into the crowd leaving my dad weeping with the tug of a Kentucky 'heart-string'. I now understand the source of my own tears in similar emotional situations.

> One of the first questions a stranger is asked in the mountains is," Where are you from?" We are oriented around places. We never forget our native places, and we go back as often as possible. A lot of us think of going back for good, perhaps to the Nolichucky, Big Sandy, Kanawha, or Oconoluftee, or Drip Rocj, Hanging Dog, Shooting Creek, Decoy, Stinking Creek, Sweetwater, or Sandy Mush. Our place is always close on our minds. 1

It was not until many years later that I came to realize that my father lived a life that totally reflected his Kentucky background. He lived a life of loving nature and couldn't get enough dirt on his hands, or fresh air in his lungs. He often talked of plant life as if it was on an equal with people. Dad tried hard to get me to identify the trees by the bark or the shape of the leaves and to memorize poetry about rivers, trees and other things that were descriptive of the nature that he loved so much. Dad loved *The Song of the Chattahoochee*, the poem written by Sidney Lanier and would often walk through the house quoting it, which would irritate me, but he would only smile real big saying how I should memorize it. Dad had a passion for people – mostly people who were earthy and for the most part poor, both in spirit and material goods but rich in faith and endowed by God's gifts of peace, humility and love. Dad took great interest in the poor, especially the African American who must have surely reminded him of his own poor background in Lawrence County, Kentucky, where he helped his family grub out a living from the poor rocky soil. Nothing can erase a few memories, which have been impressed upon my mind, no, not my mind but my very soul, for such stories have built my person, adding greatly to the gifts of God in my life. Two characters have made me what I am today – my God and my father and often it's difficult for me to tell them apart.

Over the years I have found Eastern Kentuckians to put more importance on the relationship than whatever task might be at hand. Many years after my father died Joy and I moved to Berea where we found a beautiful home with an outstanding view of the mountains and a small farm with horses grazing. To capture this view and enjoy it the remainder of our lives we sought to build an all season room on the back with a view. Of course we were eager to get it built but found that the contractor was more eager to get to know us and talk about the pride he took in building homes. We found out that he was a musician and traveled with a band but chose to give it up to spend more time with his wife and children. He wanted us to see one of his houses that he was just finishing up to see his handiwork. We shared with him that we were Kentuckians returning home after many years of being in Tennessee, Georgia, Michigan and Chicago, Illinois. It was many days of exploring together just who we were and who he was and what was possible and not possible when it came to building the addition. It was many days later that John drew up a contract and when we went over it we penciled in changes for which he commented, "We can just go ahead and sign this contract because after today no one will ever look at it." This was like saying that we had established a relationship of much more credence than what this piece of paper represented. Building a room was contingent upon building a relationship in which we understood, appreciated and trusted one another. Then and only then could the room construction begin. This was not unlike my Dad who put more importance on the relationship with the man at the service station than in the pumping of gas or receiving any kind of repair service. Once the relationship is established he could trust in the service, the ability of the people at the service station to treat him fairly and honestly.

Nothing worse could happen to the people of Appalachia than if such loyalty and trusts were to be violated. Such behavior would not be tolerated. The demonstration of such disloyalty would not only end the relationship but could well begin a feud that could last for years and result in violence. Such is the nature of the importance of relationships that exceeds any task – a task accomplished without such has no meaning. Perhaps Martin Buber says it best when he writes that all meeting is meaning and all meaning is meeting – establishing a divine-human relationship.

> Creation reveals, in meeting, its essential nature as form. It does not spill itself into expectant senses, but rises up to meet the grasping senses. The inborn *Thou* is realized in the lived relations with that which meets it. [2]

When I was about ten years old I remember being in the front yard with Dad when a black man very poorly dressed came down the street. His shoes looked as if they were about to come off his feet at every step. His clothes appeared never to have been washed. I have no idea where he was going or why he was in an all white neighborhood. I had seen black people like this in their own neighborhoods and those who came to collect the garbage on an almost daily basis. I had seen black women who worked for my mother, mostly washing clothes and cleaning the house. My rich cousins also had a black 'mammy' who stayed with them all the time. She lived up over the garage in an apartment. My cousins didn't see much of their mother for she was also the entertainer in the home and it was the 'mammy' that we related to most. Somehow that was different, even expected, but I don't think I had ever seen one just walk down our street like this before. Most of the neighbors just stared at him as if he was an alien from some distant planet. I had no idea who he was or how he got there in our neighborhood; I only know that my dad befriended him almost as if he was royalty, asking him to come sit awhile. Dad got him a drink of water and they began telling stories, laughing and enjoying one another as if they were long lost friends. Then Dad looked at the man's shoes and said. "Man, you don't have any shoe strings." In response the man answered, "Na-sah, I don't." Dad went in the house and came out with a new set of shoestrings and gave them to the man. That man was so excited! You would have thought he had been given a one hundred dollar bill!

It was not long after this that the same man came into the neighborhood again with a sack slung over his shoulder and beaming from ear to ear. He seemed to be moving so slowly. It was as if he was savoring every second of this moment as he wore a big smile and carried an obvious twinkle in his eye. He sure had the attention of us neighborhood kids as we followed him with much anticipation! He came right up to our house, took down the sack from off his shoulder and emptied out a watermelon onto the grassy lawn. By this time he had four or five of us kids around him as he broke open the melon and sat back and enjoyed watching us eat. I don't know who was the most pleased, us kids who had watermelon all over our faces and dripping from our hands down our arms and off our elbows or this beautiful black man who had a smile all over his face. I will always remember the look on his face – it was a face of a pleased man! The beatitudes began taking on a whole new meaning for me – "Blessed are the poor, for theirs is the kingdom of God." There was no question in my mind that this man was blessed; a special child of God, and furthermore my dad knew this and treated him accordingly.

It was obvious that my father had a special place in his heart for marginal people who happened to be black folk in Orlando. I'm sure this was directly related to his experience of growing up in Eastern Kentucky. If Dad had lived in South Dakota he would surely have befriended the Native American or in the inner city of Chicago it would be Mexicans, Puerto Ricans or Black Americans. It was no put on; he really identified with these people, and he had empathy for them, which drew them to him and he to them. The very last thing I remember in Orlando was Dad stopping by the place where he had worked for about ten years. In the warehouse were many blacks that Dad had come to love and they loved him. He stopped to say good-bye and I will always remember the affection that was shared at the moment of his departure. My mother would just sit in the car and wonder, "Is this move to Ashland, Kentucky necessary?" The answer was obvious – yes, it was necessary, Kentucky heartstrings were pulling and they were not to be ignored, no more than this tender moment that was launching us to a new land.

My parents took different views on this move away from Orlando. My father saw this move as another opportunity, a new adventure and as a way of getting back to his roots and family. He would be joining his brother in a new dairy business allowing him to use his bookkeeping and office experience in a new and exciting way. Mom was very distressed over this move but would go along as a dutiful spouse. My mother was comfortable in Orlando, enjoying the neighborhood and most pleased with the church we attended. She did not like Dad's family, feeling they were just too ordinary, too country and too uneducated and felt he was taking her into a situation that would make her feel misplaced and unappreciated. Of course Mom would feel this way no matter where we lived in that she was a constant worrier and carried much anxiety about her identity, or lack of, and always concerned if she was appropriate in her dress and mannerism. In other words she was extremely insecure and feared being unacceptable. No wonder she did not want to live around Dad's family in that they were most secure, never caring too much about the thoughts of others. They were just who they were, down to earth, hard working and without much formal education. As an only child Mom was doted on by her mother and told how to act and dress and how to behave, never allowing her to develop her own soul or personality. In a real sense, Mom did not know who she was.

As an adolescent, the views and attitudes of my parents concerning this move were dramatically played out in my life. At age fourteen I found this move to be a disaster and took every opportunity to express my anger toward my parents. I was extremely unhappy, moped around and made terrible grades in school. My mother took on all the blame saying we should have never moved when I was so well established in Orlando. Mother got deeper into her worrying mood and expressed much anxiety. Dad was just the opposite expressing nothing but optimism and always assuring me that everything would work out for the best. Dad allowed me to be me even when I was angrily expressing nothing but negativity.

He was an eternal optimist, never trying to change my mind while all the time assuring me that all would be well. I cannot help but reflect upon the writings of the fourteenth century Saint Julian of Norwich who from the window of her anchorhold counsel was sought by many people. Julian knew of the ravages of the Peasants' Revolt of 1381 and during these agrarian uprisings listened to tales of the world's woes, dispensing what comfort she could and sharing God's love with those who came to her.

> And so our good Lord answered to all the questions and
> doubts which I could raise, saying most comfortingly: I
> may make all things well, and I can make all things well,
> and I shall make all things well, and I will make all things
> well; and you will see yourself that every kind of thing
> will be well.... (*Showings,* p.229)

I have come to see how my father has influenced me
greatly through his patient optimism, not that I became more
patient necessarily, but because he gave me nothing to react
to negatively. Just maybe nothing is permanent, only
impermanence, and my present situation would soon pass.
Just because it's a dark cloudy rainy day does not mean the
sun has disappeared forever; the clouds will move on and the
sun will shine again. Dad's attitude was a real blessing to me
that I never came to appreciate until many years later.

These were bittersweet moments, experiences I would
never forget; experiences that were to have their beginnings
and endings in Appalachia all because of a father that never
forgot his roots. Beginnings of joy filled with friends–a
neighborhood where I was joined and disjointed, experiences
of joy and sadness that I embrace lest I forget who and
whose I am, as I continue my journey, but not without
framing my childhood in a manner that becomes a window
in which to view my developing soul.

Some years ago there was a popular book, at least with
those of us who were seeking personal/spiritual growth,
entitled *If You Meet the Buddha on the Road, Kill Him.* 3 As
we journey there is no one authority, charismatic leader or
personality that holds all the truth, but rather we must find
our own way of "enlightenment" taking seriously all our
experiences along the way, claiming them as our own – both
the good, the bad and the indifferent. And often the journey
can take strange twists and turns as we reach back to reach
forward – life runs shallow without embracing both genesis
and exodus. The calling takes many forms.

Perhaps the greatest calling of all is to be comfortable in our own skin. To be at home or at rest within ourselves is a gift that allows us peace and joy wherever we might travel or find ourselves. I can never recall my father complaining about the meals my mother prepared. If my brother and I were to complain he would only reply, "Be thankful for what you have. Your mother has worked hard to prepare good meals and we should learn to enjoy what she has put before us." Of course I can never recall my father complaining about anything. He was most unusual in this manner.

We always ate meals together as a family. It was something my mother insisted upon even though my brother and I found it to be an inconvenience at times. As I look back on this I find it was a manner in which we could be at home with one another. A time to share and experience one another that was not possible at any other time. One of my fondest memories at the dinner table was when my father kept looking curiously at his salad. Mother would often wash off a head of lettuce and quarter it for the four of us and place it on a small side plate. We could then put our choice of mayonnaise or dressing on the salad, cut it up and eat it. My father continued to stare at the lettuce with this puzzling look. Mother said, 'Frank is there something wrong with your lettuce?' Dad responded with, 'Oh no, it's O.K.' But Dad continued this strange behavior and avoided cutting into his lettuce. Mom then became persistent and all but demanded that Dad tell her what was the problem with his food. He responded, saying, 'There is a frog in my lettuce." Mom jumped up and pulled his lettuce apart and there was a tiny green frog in the lettuce. We all laughed and laughed. Mom said, 'Just how long would you have stared at that frog without saying anything?'

Dad took life as it came, frog and all. This story is the epitome of my father. He and Saint Julian of Norwich would hit it off well, offering up assurance that all was well.

KENTUCKY HEARTSTRINGS

Molded and shaped with passion
much like the artisan.
gouging, pushing and pulling,
mastering the clay
while Kentucky heartstrings
lie inviting.

The tapestry is woven
but left incomplete
with loose threads that wait,
waiting for the final journey
the road home,
beginning with the pulling
of the Kentucky heartstrings.

Many experience the heart
especially the poor,
those who have been there,
longing for the early foggy mornings
that gives way to the sun –
all pulling the heartstrings
of their favorite son.

ON HOLY GROUND

Inquisitive
Turning aside
Being distracted
Seeing the unusual
You are on holy ground

Listening to the unspoken
Staring out the window
Into unimaginable possibilities
Hearing voices
You are on holy ground

Questioning logic
Loving solitude
Shoes off
Lost in candle flame
You are on holy ground

Not crazy
Yet perhaps a fool for Christ

"Christianity has taken a giant stride into the absurd. Remove from Christianity its ability to shock and it is altogether destroyed. It then becomes a tiny superficial thing, capable neither of inflicting deep wounds nor of healing them."

Soren Kierkegaard

Where is the wise man? Where is the scribe? Where is the debater of this age? Has not God made foolish the wisdom of the world? For the foolishness of God is wiser than man, and the weakness of God is stronger than men.

I Corinthians 1:20,25

STREET PREACHER

He was a big man, with grimy overalls, and hair that dangled over his eyes and down the back of his neck. He always wore a plaid long-sleeved shirt regardless of the weather; it could be in the nineties and yet he would have on that same shirt. His eyes seemed intent on something we could not see. Even in his wildest moments, his eyes seemed to speak of more than what was visible. To stop and listen to him felt like joining a crowd looking up at the sky only to feel like a fool when nothing was up there to see; and yet we might say to ourselves, "Or was there?" That was the way this street preacher could make me feel. What's he looking at? What am I missing? Does he see something I don't? There must be something to this man beyond the dirt and apparent disregard for appearance, but what could it possibly be? I kind of wanted to continue "staring into the sky" at moments like these, but knew others might think I too was crazy. Is there really any difference?

I often think our western perspective blinds us. Our education from kindergarten is so highly shaped by the rational and logical that I have sometimes felt ashamed of using my imagination or feeling things deeply that is impossible to explain rationally. The period of the Enlightenment and Reformation all but removed mystery from our western education, to the point that almost everything must be explained; it has to make sense logically or it's dismissed as a useless thought or idea. I have experienced this all my life and especially during my formal education. In junior high school I would sit in class and look out the window with my mind full of dreams and ideas that excited and intrigued me. The teacher wrote to my mother, "Tommy doesn't pay attention, he only wants to stare out the window." I found that the view out the window was far more interesting than the dry, boring mathematical problem she was putting on the board. Never did I have a teacher seriously ask me what I was looking at or thinking. Perhaps this is what interested me most about this street preacher – no one was giving him the time of day, only writing him off as of no value to our rational world.

I always admired people who could be "holy," which in the New Testament Greek means "different," not for the sake of being different but because they feel called out or separated for a spiritual purpose. The Russian Orthodox Church especially understands this idea and holds folk in high esteem who are "holy," referring to them as "Fools for Christ."[1] It takes a special kind of person to be foolish in this sense, a person with deep faith in God. I like to think that this street preacher was just such a person, sort of "in the world but not of the world." I was always amazed at how folk in Jackson could just go on their way as if he was not even there in spite of his large physique and loud voice, a dominating presence in this small town in Eastern Kentucky. Yet to give this man their attention would mean they would have to take themselves seriously on a deeper level than most of us find comfortable. We learn to dismiss such people, projecting on them our own spiritual foolishness, and passively letting them bear that which we would rather not look at or claim within ourselves. As long as we have archetypal figures like street preachers to carry these issues we can go on our way, however, not without great loss of soul.

> Make no mistake about it: if any one of you thinks of himself as wise, in the ordinary sense of the world, then he must learn to be a fool before he really can be wise. 2

I Corinthians 3.18

The street preacher would often be close to the Breathitt County Court House, a big four story brick building that seemed to be the hub of much activity. Many outlaws who made a name for themselves in the Wild West were originally from this area, and their exploits helped give it the nickname "Bloody Breathitt." The old courthouse was filled with bullet holes both inside and out from those days. When they decided to build a new courthouse a portion of the funding came from the sale of bullet-riddled bricks and boards from the old courthouse. People took great pride in such relics, which made wonderful conversation pieces. It was not unusual to visit in a home and see a brick displayed proudly on the mantle or some other conspicuous place just waiting to tell its story. Most of the stories had some historical basis, but each time the story was told it got just a little longer and a little further from the truth. This was generally understood, and yet people continued to enjoy the telling and listening to such tales. Outside the old courthouse men sat on boxes or benches chewing and spitting tobacco and whittling. It was not unusual for many of these men to stay there everyday, all day, just "spit'in and whit'lin". Conversation often revolved around their knives, where they got them, how long they had had a particular knife and the quality of steel in various knives. Trading knives became story telling time, seeing who could tell the best lie about a knife while the shavings and the spit flew. While some of the men were quite artistic, carving figures of various sorts, most just whittled, leaving giant piles of wood shavings at their feet. This was the best entertainment mainly because it was the only entertainment in town, except for basketball – a sport that more resembled a religion.

I never dreamed I would ever end up in a community like Jackson, and yet here I was along with my family. My whole family! When I was accepted at Lee's Junior College and they found out my father was an accountant they wanted him to come and run the business office almost sight unseen. It was difficult getting good people to come to Eastern Kentucky, but Dad, being an Eastern Kentuckian himself, got excited about this job and so the two of us started college together, so to speak. I had no college and had just barely gotten through high school. I had tried to get into other colleges but no one would even think about taking me with my poor academic background. Lee's took just about anyone who wanted to get an education. The college's sole purpose was to provide an education to mountain people who had limited resources, both academically and financially.

My mother was not happy about this move, but as a good wife she went along in support of my father. Mom was an only child who was raised in a city much larger than Jackson. To Mom, Jackson was one trashy place; she considered it little more than a mission field where she would have to put in time. Of course the duration of time they would spend in Jackson was never established, especially since Dad enjoyed his work as well as the people; Mom could never understand or appreciate the place or the people. Jackson was just too threatening or "shadowy" and she was too clean to appreciate anything that looked dark, dirty, and had no intentions of changing even if it meant the loss of soul. She felt toward the whole town of Jackson about the way most people felt toward the street preacher – trash to be avoided.

"The shadow" which represents the unconscious is a rich

concept developed by Carl Gustav Jung. It is the shadow that contains evil, yet 98% is gold, according to Jung; we just perceive it as evil. We seek either to deny the shadow material or project it onto others keeping us from dealing constructively with our unconscious. Connie Zweig and Steve Wolf believe it is important to romance the shadow or to befriend it in such a way that it is no longer denied, disowned, rejected or projected onto others.3 From a spiritual and psychological perspective denial or projection of the shadow keeps us from wholeness or completeness hindering us from loving our neighbors as ourselves.

In Jungian psychology and spiritual thought we learn that such shadow material becomes a trash can for our psyche, a place where we can project, or dump, all that which we dislike about ourselves, rather than deal with it in any constructive manner. I have learned that anytime a person, a group of people or a place is distasteful or threatening to me, I had best pay attention. It just may be that such reactions are telling me more about myself than the negative feelings are telling me about others. When we react so strongly we had best take notice. This is a difficult lesson to learn; I suspect most of us keep harboring resentments and wounds with which we dare not deal, as long as we have a shadow to trash. Who wants to deal with their trash when they can find others to carry it, be it the street preacher, Jackson or anyone different from us.

One day the street preacher was thumbing a ride, and I picked him up on my way home. I can't remember what we talked about as I drove through this beautiful hilly country with the winding roads shaded by large trees that came right to the edge of the pavement. All of a sudden the street preacher shouted out, "Stop the car!" I stopped immediately. The preacher was looking back over his shoulder and with great enthusiasm said, "Back up!" I backed up to a beautiful shaded hollow that ran up between two mountains, where he told me to stop. With much passion he looked up this numinous hollow filled with mysterious shadows, as the sun barely streaked through the thickly forested area, and said, "You see this place? This is where you can talk with God." He didn't say anything else which at the time seemed peculiar because on the street he talked nonstop and with great volume. I could only guess that this was a place of great awe where the street preacher came to get renewed; a place that fed his soul and renewed his spirit. A place where God was calling – 'Come sit a spell', an Appalachian solace for the soul. Perhaps this is how the street preacher could continue his ministry in an indifferent world.

The Celtic tradition describes places or experiences where heaven and earth come together as "thin places." These evoke something spiritual in people just as the smell of burning leaves can bring back childhood memories. When I was in Ireland I was with a group studying water from the mystically spiritual perspective. Our travels took us to various wells and springs that had a history of deep spiritual significance. Over the centuries people had come and continue to come in search of healing, for themselves or for someone else. These springs and wells were known for their power even before Christianity was known in the land. Wells were "thin places" respected by Celtic people.

I will never forget this experience nor will I forget this man who knew God and shared with me this thin place, a place too holy for words, a place that left even a street preacher speechless. I often wonder if this place is not only a place to talk with God but also what is more important a place to be still and listen to God.

Listening is a gift that comes to only a few. I once heard a psychiatrist say, "If you can find someone who will listen to you, you best beat a path to her or his door." I have often thought about this statement and have become increasingly convinced of its truth. When I was director of the Pastoral Counseling Center in Savannah, Georgia a dear friend gave me a framed cross stitch she had made which reads, "Called to listen to the needs of others, even those unspoken." I wouldn't take anything for her gift; it has been hanging on my office wall for years. If I were to change anything about this statement I would substitute "especially" for "even," because the unspoken need often holds more meaning and potential for growth.

Street preacher taught me that if you are going to have anything to say you had best first learn how to listen. I would have never guessed this wisdom could come from a man who preached so hard and so long, a dirty, uneducated man who was often passed by. However, I have not found his wisdom in the church, at least the Protestant Church as I have experienced it. Pastors in the institutional church are too quick to pray. Not only are pastors quick to pray but the prayers are too polished and thought out especially in situations outside the formal worship setting. I have often seen prayer used as a controlling device to control or limit conversation. Often I think pastors listen to others with prayer in mind as if to say, "How am I going to put this into a prayer?" This thinking limits or even prevents listening. Are we just as quick to listen as to pray? Perhaps instead of placing so much stress on prayer we need to put more emphasis on listening. I think if I were in need of prayer I would first hope to be listened to and then and, only then, have someone say a verbal prayer for me. Even more important would be to find a quiet place to listen and contemplate with God's will in mind. In our society it is difficult to listen because it seems a far too passive way of responding and it places our concerns in God's time and not on our hurried schedule. Most of us are far too active for this; we want to take charge, have our prayers and move on. Perhaps the most important question for us today is, "Has anyone heard from the Lord?" A second important question is, "Do you have a place to listen?"

At the First Presbyterian Church in Arlington Heights, Illinois I often complained that the complex had no holy place – no quiet area designated for prayer and meditation. Even in the sanctuary one cannot pull aside to be quiet or to just listen. This church is probably no different from many churches that emphasize programmatic activities that are extremely extraverted leaving little space that is not filled with much talking, laughter, or singing. There is nothing wrong with such activities; they are most enjoyable to the majority of our society. The complaint I have is that there is not equal respect, with designated space, for the more introverted person who needs solitude and quiet to be energized for ministry. A Quaker friend once told me when non-Quakers attend a meeting they often don't know what to expect and become anxious. Ten to fifteen minutes into the silent meeting such visitors might ask, "When does the service begin?" at which time the Quakers respond, "When worship is over."

The story of Moses has always intrigued me for it is a story that so well illustrates the theme of listening versus our own busy, controlling lives. Moses had tried to take control of the situation in Egypt and let his anger get the best of him. Moses' anger at the Egyptians for enslaving his people led to his murdering an Egyptian who was beating a Hebrew (Exodus 3:11). Moses then fled for his life into the land of Midian where he married and lived as a shepherd. It was in this pastoral setting that he heard God. Moses put himself, perhaps unknowingly, into a position or place where God could show himself, be known and speak. Moses made himself available. Then God made himself known, as visible words, through a "burning bush." It is as if seeing adds something to hearing. I can't help but note that it was Moses who "turned aside" to see this great sight – God got his attention. As a result of this experience Moses was then "called" to be a prophet – a leader of his people.

Moses is an archetype for the street preacher for each man learned how to retreat and put himself in a place where God could speak to him – whether in a desert or a hollow deep between two mountains. The street preacher made himself available to God, and then and only then was he equipped for ministry – to preach. Listening comes first and then prayerful action in the world.

During my clinical training I was engaged with a number of people who were in painful situations and institutionalized with various diagnoses, medical terms that often were little more than name-calling. I knew when I had genuinely heard a client when I felt a presence that was more than the two of us. I was aware of an unavoidable transcendence that I could only define as God. I would often ask the patient, "Do you feel we are on holy ground and that our conversation has been a kind of prayer with God listening carefully to our thoughts and feelings?" Usually they would agree and would share with me other such experiences. Before leaving the room I would say, "In that God has been with us in our conversation perhaps we need only say, 'Amen.' To offer a formal prayer with eyes shut and hands folded would be unnecessary, invalidating the very presence of God that we had just experienced. Again I am reminded of Martin Buber and the gift he has given to us all in his theological concept of "I and Thou." Instead of treating persons and the natural world as useful tools for furthering our own ends (an "I and it" mentality), Buber exhorts us to respect the worth and the being of other persons and the creation. Do we, like Buber, Moses or the street preachers have the ability to "turn aside" and recognize the holy within and among us? I strongly feel we must learn to be inquisitive, easily distracted by the unusual and listeners to the unspoken if we are to engage in a divine-human dialogue.

Isn't it interesting how experiences we don't really understand at the moment, can be forever imprinted upon our minds? This is certainly the case with the street preacher and me. This man was no doubt an introvert. My journey has brought me to appreciate terms "introvert" and "extrovert," terms coined by the Swiss psychiatrist C.G. Jung. Jung tells us that introvertedness and extrovertedness are means by which we become energized. Being around many people energizes an extroverted person. The extrovert seems to thrive on parties and interacting with many people. Yet with introverts it is just the opposite; they become energized through being alone or one on one with another person. Often they take a nap, listen to music or pull aside in silence. The introvert seems to have a deep spiritual center that must be nourished, which in retrospect I see in this street preacher. This is why he got so excited and yet reverent when he saw the hollow. Surely the hollow was the place where he got refueled or spiritually energized, which allowed him to preach on the street with such enthusiasm.

As I think upon this theme another archetype comes to mind for the street preacher. I envision John the Baptist being such a person, a true introvert with a deep spiritual center that thrived upon the quiet, deserted wilderness of Judea. It was in such a deserted place that John would recharge his batteries for the next day of hard preaching of hell, fire and brimstone. I can envision the street preacher and John being a whole lot alike – dirty, loud, smelly and all but just living off the land. Not exactly what you would expect a messenger from the Lord to look like and yet God has chosen some mighty peculiar people to deliver his message: such as Isaiah (Isaiah 20:3) who ran naked through the streets of Jerusalem, Hosea who was married to a whore (Hosea1:2-3), and Moses who was a murderer (Exodus 2:11-12.) My father would often say to me, "Tom, everyone is peculiar, just some more peculiar than others." So it is, and yet, why does it seem that God uses the most peculiar to reveal his message?

It would be a spell before I was to return to this part of the country, and I did not realize at the time how my life was being shaped and formed by encounters in the Eastern Kentucky Mountains. Threads of such experiences have been woven into my life unaware, forming and shaping my soul. Because they are part of me I cannot lose them; instead I spread out the fabric and marvel at patterns that have only revealed them in retrospect.

While working as a Chaplain Intern at Georgia Mental

Health Institute in Atlanta I enjoyed the patients that remained a mystery, defying all diagnoses. Although labels had to be placed upon them or in their charts, which I always referred to as name calling – schizophrenics, bi-polars, etc. To me they were God's children trying to find their place in the world like all the rest of us. I enjoyed the patient that liked living in 'thin places', that would search the sky, and wonder, to look out windows with no rational explanation of why or what they expected to see or find.

I will always remember Ms. Davis who was so proud of a certificate of ordination she carried with her and would show it to you whether or not you were interested. This certificate had been folded and unfolded so many times it was in shreds. I knew she was a candidate for sabotaging a religious service I provided for the patients. It was always a challenge and Ms. Davis did not let me down. Sure enough she took over the service with her preaching and praying leading only to chaos and a quick dismissal of the service. A few days later I was paged to come to the patient lounge where I found Ms. Davis preaching to the patients. The look on the faces of the patients demonstrated nothing but anger and short fuses that were too soon to explode. I had experienced the street preacher and now I was experiencing the mental institution preacher both with the same goal of saving souls but in a different setting with a different audience. I came up beside Ms. Davis and said, "Ms. Davis what is going on?" She quickly responded, heavily panting, saying, "They are all going to hell and I have got to preach them into heaven." With which I replied with a loud voice, "Praise the Lord!" Ms. Davis threw her arms around me and with great strength she whirled us around and around. When she stopped she let out a great sigh and walked into her room and fell onto her bed. Ms. Davis got her convert and with much joy and satisfaction was now at rest.

On this adult psychiatric unit I also had the experience of meeting one of the patients recently admitted who for some unknown reason was constantly walking. Up and down the unit floor and around the nurse's station he walked. I walked with him, with no conversation, until at last he decided to stop and laid flat on his back in the middle of the floor. I laid beside him silently listening to our heavy breathing while staring at the ceiling. After a few minutes I expressed how restful it was just lying on the floor resting after such a vigorous walk. My comment was followed with more silence yet after just a few moments he rose and went to his room where he rested in his bed.

Now there was silence, there was peace and there was rest. Indeed roads do run backwards as well as forward with memories merging carrying us through various holy grounds, finding faith to live by and hope to thrive. Silence might often appear to be nonproductive in an industrial society and yet silence just might be the only way and most likely the best way to communicate. Better yet silence is often the preparation for more outward productivity and healthy creativity. The Street Preacher knew this well when he silently listened in a holy place, a hollow in the mountains of Appalachia. Just perhaps the silently walking patient was experiencing much of the same in his own manner.

It seems to me that silence can be used in different ways. First, silence can be a means for focusing on a particular issue or subject. A group might get together to contemplate on a passage or verse of Scripture. This might be followed up with group discussion with everyone having a chance to express what they had contemplated during the silent time together. Second, silence can be a useful tool for prayer. One finds silence in order to be more open to the Other – a means by which to be spiritually nurtured or empowered. This could have been the purpose of silence in the hollow for the Street Preacher, a place to become empowered by God in order to continue his ministry on the street. His purpose is to listen for a message from God. Third, silence is used as a means for meditation in which one has no purpose other than to be present in the moment.

But how do we go about becoming silent? Morton Kelsey says it is a process of learning to be alone and quiet.

> This is the beginning of silence, of the process of introversion. .... This means shutting out the invading noises from both the outside world and the inner psychic one. To become really silent, one has to come to a halt outwardly at the same time. It is very much like thinking about getting a car tuned up while roaring down the freeway. One cannot do much about it until one slows down, pulls into a service station, and turns off the motor. In reality, this idea of stopping the wheels of progress periodically for silence is universally common in spiritual practice. 4

It must be noted that this process is much easier for the introvert who already feels at home in silence.

> For the extrovert, silence means an about face or turning away from a part of life that seems valuable and familiar. The difficulty for introverts is in stepping out of themselves, in reaching out, say, to a stranger in church or at a swimming pool. Turning toward an inner world is just as difficult for the extrovert and also just as necessary and valuable. Both are as vital to full Christian life as the two halves of a beating heart. But today's world applauds our efforts to reach out, forgetting that those efforts require an inner basis that is anchored in silence and that something happens in silence. 5

LISTEN TO THE SILENCE

Listen to the silence
that catches a mountain stream
moving through the sky like a cloud,
with the bliss of the day dream
no need to speak out loud.

Be still and know
silence runs deep
as a language forgotten yet speaks
often within our sleep –
inherit the earth with the meek.

More than the absence of sound,
listen to the silence, as
leaves falling on an autumn day,
a world bent on violence,
the poor crying for more say.

Fear not silence
for it is a better way.
Be not afraid to listen,
silence will have its say,
the soul it will awaken.

APPALACHIAN WINTER

Twisting and turning,
among hills that glisten and sparkle,
an early wintry morn –
God's ice covered creation.
Sun not yet burning
yet streaking through valleys,
illuminating narrow mountain roads as
ice covers deep scars allowing
only beauty of this Appalachian trail.

"...a spiritual wound is not to be confused with a neurosis or crippling injury. It is not a limited wound, but a wound through which pours the life of God."

John A. Sanford

BACK AGAIN

Twisting and turning from out of the peaks and valleys of the Appalachian Mountains come the three rivers flowing past abandoned farms, rusted out cars and wild flowers; Beattyville passively waiting in silence as three tributaries merge forming the Kentucky River. Once again I find myself in this rugged terrain as if drawn by an Appalachian father. Somehow, returning to these hills is as natural as rain on a spring day and yet I question, wondering, why I would want to minister in this place, like a toy that has been used and abused by many children and now placed on a shelf, gathering dust and all but ignored. As one drives between, around and over these rugged mountains it's difficult not to feel the wounds of this country and it's people. Often referred to as a depressed area and yet so much more. Barefoot children with dirty faces playing in grassless yards while "soup" beans simmer on top of a pot bellied stove, and yet so much more. A little red elementary school overshadowed by a giant basketball coliseum, but so much more. Just perhaps it is this 'so much more' that draws me into these hills again; that which one can feel only with heart and soul, an experience that cannot be put into words. Ask most anyone in these parts about this 'so much more' and they will agree its here, but don't ask them to explain the unexplainable.

I reckon when one reaches out to distant lands and becomes disillusioned, confused and generally pissed-off at life, one retreats back to the familiar and the comfortable. Looking back, this is what I did after working for a year in Michigan as Minister of Youth and Christian Education. That seems so far off and so long ago. Kentucky was home for my wife, Joy, and me; Joy, home grown in Lawrence County, along with ten siblings. Eastern Kentucky was no stranger to me and had been my home, my mentor and my heart in many ways. Attending Lee's Junior College in 'Bloody' Breathitt was an education in itself even if you never opened a book.

The sleepy town of Beattyville, deep in the hills of Lee County was always waiting, as was all of Eastern Kentucky, for anyone with an education. Good doctors, lawyers and preachers were hard to come by and then they had the tendency not to stay very long. I'm not even sure you had to be good at what you did as long as you had the education and credentials for the task at hand. In this part of the country folk were just glad to get any kind of professional. I can remember an Elder of the church taking me to the bank shortly after I arrived in town and introducing me to the president of the bank, as well as the most prestigious layperson in the Episcopal Church, whose pulpit had been vacant for a long time. The Episcopal congregation had a priest who came in from Lexington on Sunday mornings to perform the clerical duties for morning worship. Elder McLean placed his hands in his pockets and reared back with a big smile on his face as he said, "Well, we got our'n, when you gonna get your'n? The Presbyterians had completed their task and got a preacher and they were going to show him off.

I was warmly welcomed in this community; however, I knew I would never be accepted as one of them. I would always be a foreigner. To be a native it helped if you were born in the county or at least had deep family roots; someone's son or daughter who was raised on a particular ridge or up a known hollow. Family is as important as the very air one breathes; it gives sustenance, as does the earth to the trees that stand tall only by the roots running deep. One is usually identified by one's daddy – "You're Jake Turner's son, ain't ye?" Loyal Jones tells of two mountaineers talking of their kin folk saying, "You know he is a real S.O.B. The other replied, 'Yeah, but he's our S.O.B.'

Henry Combs was a sociology professor at Lee's Junior College who was deeply submerged into the Eastern Kentucky culture. I just couldn't help but think of Henry as I again found myself in these hills that pull on my heart. Henry, just by watching you walk and talk, could tell you the county in which you and your family were from, and if he knew your name it was a dead give away. Professor Combs loved to engage with the freshman class each year at which time he would call the class role and after each name would say what county you were from and many times could tell you the name of your daddy. 'Foreigners' found this amazing while the natives were entertained but not at all surprised. All the natives knew Turners came from Breathitt County, Brandenburgs from Lee County and Gabbards from Owsley County. It was just common knowledge, yet it was refreshing to hear Henry identify the freshman class. Henry Combs affirmed students from Eastern Kentucky as if to legitimize him or her by establishing them to a proper place, with legitimate family, by the principle of hereditary rights in a land that had many bastard qualities. Anyone who has any kind of identity or roots in Eastern Kentucky will find it difficult to totally detach. Jobs may be secured in Ohio while cars were worn out on the highways heading back for the weekends. I have some appreciation of this longing for the hills, for here I am again, like a homecoming, and yet my roots don't run nearly as deep. When the mountain parkway was built during Governor Combs' reign people often referred to it as a way out, but it became, just as importantly, a way back home.

The Manse (Scottish Presbyterian for parsonage) sat up

on a rise from off the Booneville highway. Across the road was a view of an overgrown and neglected field with a small pond lying deep in a ravine. Beattyville lay low in the valley where the three rivers came together, and to get to Booneville it was necessary to wind up a steep hill until you got to the top, right where the Presbyterian manse was located. It was at the top of this hill where the road stretched out from all its twisting and climbing, the very place where speed could be regained for a good distance before the road began curving again. In this hill country many drivers took advantage of a straight road and often would see how fast they could drive. One cannot be too careful. I once came around a curve in a nearby county to find two men working on their car in the middle of the highway. In this part of the country the highway can become the only place to work on a car. This is especially true if your house butts up against a mountain with the front yard sloping to the highway. The road then becomes like your private drive, of a sorts. These two men actually had their car jacked up and doing what looked like some major repair. And on another occasion while driving at night I found a herd of cows in the road. I followed these cows for miles before they found a place to move off the highway, allowing me to pass. In this part of the country the highway can often be used as an extension of one's driveway or pasture. Back again to a land and a people who have their own peculiar ways, ways that must be honored and respected and even learned from if possible. Anything less is only to make life miserable in this often forgotten land. The first time I found myself in these parts was to seek an education, which might seem like an oxymoron. Normally one would not seek out an education in Eastern Kentucky; however, things were different for me. Yale, Duke nor even the University of Kentucky were not an option for me at the time; and yet as I look back on my first experience in Breathitt County at the little Lee's Junior College, neither of these larger institutions could give me the experience I needed at the time for a well-rounded education. I figure just about anyone can get a formal education which mostly amounts to memorizing what the professor or books are saying and then learn how to feed it back to them for a good grade. Do this enough and you get a piece of paper called a diploma which, in return, you can get hired on somewhere as an expert. Surely this is nothing more than regurgitation education; take it in, chew it up and spit it back for a good grade and become an expert. I did just enough of this to get me where I felt I was called to be – in ministry. So much of this is a game to be played while real education comes from experience, learning from the living documents of life. It took me a long time to learn this. My real education has come from that which my father would call "hard knocks", – encountering the real world and learning lessons that are often hidden from our western academic orientation.

I had been pretty much beat up in Michigan by the pastor of the church where I was called to work with the youth from a highly structured community where people were extremely task-success oriented and ordered their lives accordingly. The pastor was narcissistic and threatened by most any recognition or acceptance that I received from members of the congregation. Preachers need a good dose of narcissism in order to get up and preach each Sunday but this man had way too much, exceeding the necessary requirement for effective preaching. And now I am back again to regain my focus in order to continue my journey. Beattyville would be refreshing in that it would allow me the space and time to refocus and find the direction I needed to take in my ministry. I, or anyone else, did not consciously speak of my need; there was no reason to do so; these folks were just glad to get a young pastor under most any circumstances. It was pretty well understood that any young pastor coming to these two small churches would likely not stay long before they would move on in their ministry. In fact this is one of the greatest services that small churches offer to the larger church and yet they get little credit or recognition.

Back again or am I just passing through to another place? Whatever the case it appears a necessary process for my spiritual journey. One of the most beautiful experiences of my life was driving one early wintry morning while ice covered the valleys and hills making even the scars of this land beautiful if only for a moment. This experience is analogous to my life in many ways, having moments of elation even, and especially, in times of disillusionment. I had returned to Kentucky having completed my formal education and experienced a horrendous year in a church in Michigan. I was no longer sure the church was where I needed to be. Perhaps I was in the wilderness of my ministry. Floundering around looking for a direction, unsure if I had anything to offer in the desert of my life, just hoping that I might come to see something more than just a mirage.

It was years before I was to realize that I was right where I needed to be spiritually, emotionally and socially. I was in a community that allowed me to be me, bad sermons and all. I was in a supportive marriage that gave me the necessary space that I needed before moving on to a different place in my life. The only pressure that I felt was the pressure that I put on myself. Yes, I was back again to a familiar place, a safe place where wounds could heal – a spiritual place that would leave an eternal impression upon my soul.

I will be forever thankful for the friendship and wisdom of Sylvia Brinton Perera with whom I had the privilege to travel in Ireland. Sylvia's writings speak to the very depth of my soul especially as I think back on my days of floundering in Eastern Kentucky. Sylvia writes of the Irish Goddess Maeve as the powerful "displayed woman" in Celtic lore seen as sculptures on medieval French and British churches and Irish castles portraying a female with legs spread.

> Worldwide from the Paleolithic period on, the birth-giving mother has been depicted as a powerful "displayed woman" with upraised hands, prominent navel, with her open legs revealing her huge genitals. Called by their Irish name, Sheela-na-gig. Over church windows and on graveyards where they join the taking of life to the giving of life, the huge genitalia of the displayed woman open to

reveal the power of the vulva as an entrance to tomb and womb. Thus the figures force the worshipper to consider the mystery of death and renewal both in this world and projected onto the next. As a divine mystery, the sacred body of the goddess then represents the source from which we emerge and in which we find our rest – the source that creates, motivates, sustains, regenerates, and receives back all life. Focus on the dark vulva makes the figure a monstrance of the origin and goal of transformation. 1

I have found that most people resist moving into a dark period of their lives. Denial is so much a part of our lives that we will not allow anything negative, dark, painful or depressive to enter our consciousness. We are programmed to be happy all the time. This is one major reason many people will not read the paper, feeling it is too negative and filled with bad news of people being killed, divorced, raped, etc. Our affluent culture will not allow us to claim our dark side but rather dictates that we be happy, portraying lives that demonstrate that we have it 'all together'. This was clearly seen with a wealthy family in a Chicago suburb. The husband and father of three small children left his wife and children in an enormous house located in a high-class neighborhood. The wife, in a state of depression, killed all her children and attempted on her own life. It was clear that this woman was unable to live under such dark conditions and had to take these drastic actions rather than to retreat into the darkness of the tomb, the dark vulva that makes possible the goal of transformation. There is a tremendous price to pay when we fail to take seriously our darkness, allowing it into our consciousness that we might become more whole. Sue Monk Kid suggests that such darkness could possibly be referred to as a 'holy dark', a place to incubate, creating the necessary space or womb for development or rebirth. 2

This has also become true of the cultural music of the African-American, the blues. A *Mother Jones* article asks some good questions. "Whose music is the blues? How did the blues, a serious form of expression rooted in the hard life of marginalized people, become a good-time music for moneyed tourists? What's left of the strange and unique power of the blues?" Honeyboy Edwards, a living legend at the age of 'Eighty-Eight', and still plays up to fifty gigs a year, gives us the answer.

> I'll tell you how the blues started," Edwards said, his hands folded neatly on his lap. "It came from our side of the world. The blues started from slavery, by people working in slavery. They started to holler songs, and they hollered all day to make the day pass by quickly. That's how the blues started, and it's been the blues ever since. 3

The people of Appalachia have a lot in common with their ancient ancestors in Ireland and the African American who know how to claim their darkness that life might prevail. These mountain people know the true meaning of baptism, a sense of going under the water or being swallowed by the darkness of the vulva or tomb of the great mother. They know how to sing of their plight and weariness just as the African Americans know how to claim their pain and suffering dating back to a time of slavery. For the Appalachian, life cannot be denied, but fully grasped if they are to survive with any hope of transformation; but to the outsider it might only appear as gloom and doom. Too many in America have forgotten the meaning of spiritual woundedness and how to genuinely claim it for the renewal of the soul. In the *Mother Jones* article by David Hajdu sited above we read,

> 2003 is the "Year of the Blues." But as a music born of oppression becomes a feel-good soundtrack for white America, just what are we celebrating?

This statement could just as easily apply to traditional mountain music, which has been made over for those who would rather not look at pain and suffering and bury them in pop cultured country music. The following lyric to an old Appalachian song is telling of how mountain folk express their woundedness in music.

Come all ye fair and tender ladies

Take warning how you court your men

They're like a star on a summer morning

They first appear and then they're gone

They'll tell to you some loving story

And they'll make you think that they love you well

And away they'll go and court some other

And leave you there in grief to dwell

I wish I was a little sparrow

And I had wings to fly so high

I'd fly to the arms of my false true lover

And when he'd ask, I would deny

Oh love is handsome, love is charming

And love is pretty while it's new

But love grows cold as love grows older

And fades away like morning dew 4

Joan and Duane Kauffman have been working tirelessly in Harlan, Kentucky for many years with the mentally ill. They are good friends who often share their work and ministry – a ministry that knows the pain and suffering of the mountain people. Duane and Joan have come to love these people just as they are, without expecting them to be or become anything more than they are – depressed, lonely and suffering. Joan once said to me, "There is no church in which the mentally ill can feel welcome."

Where is the church in which the wounded can sing *Fair*

and Tender Ladies? In what church can the depressed and lonely weep and express their anger? Just one day a year do we dare speak of death and dying and that is only in a historical context called "Good Friday" and then we gloss over it quickly. Easter and Christmas come much too soon for many of God's suffering children. The church too often wants to "save" people before they can be found or perhaps accepted for who they are and integrated as equals among all God's people.

While serving as a pastoral counselor in a large church I found wounded people who were grieving the loss of a loved one, others who were unacceptable for their sexual orientation and still others who could not move beyond their shame and guilt. Many felt the church only added to their pain expecting them somehow to 'get over it' and to 'be happy.' In some cases the church expects salvation and baptism to somehow magically cure individuals of their personal woundedness and when it doesn't work out this way they feel guilty. I started a "Blue Christmas Service" which was held approximately one week before Christmas Day encouraging all the wounded, the guilty, the angry, the homeless, the mentally ill and the grieving to join me and the other pastors for a service in which we would take seriously their woundedness. A Blue Christmas Service embraces pain at the time of the year when our culture is especially suppressing pain through bright lights, laughter and celebration. I have had people after the service say to me, "Thanks for giving me closure." Others expressed hope amid the blueness in that it endorsed or validated them in a culture or family or church which otherwise ignored them or placed upon them unrealistic expectations. A spiritual community is one in which the gifts of God are being poured out through the wounded if only we will make it possible.

> When we see a woman and her child begging on the street, when we see a man mercilessly beating his terrified dog, when we see a teenager who has been badly beaten or see fear in the eyes of a child, do we turn away because we

can't bear it? Most of us probably do. Someone needs to encourage us not to brush aside what we feel, not to be ashamed of the love and grief it arouses in us, not to be afraid of pain. Some one needs to encourage us that this soft spot in us could be awakened and that to do this would change our lives. **4**

I had made almost a full circle, from Breathitt County where I attended a small Presbyterian Junior College to Lee County, just next door. I thought I was ready for ministry, and perhaps I was, except I was now called on more to be a social worker. Oh, I think I had this soft spot that was awakened which was becoming a problem. Just how many problems can there be and how much help is enough?

One of the Elders called saying his brother was just being released from jail and would I go down and talk with him. The brother had been in jail for drunkenness. We talked for a while when he asked if I would come by his trailer for a visit, after he had a chance to clean up a bit. I waited a few hours and then went to his trailer. I knocked on the door and he called out for me enter. I took a chair just in front of the couch where he was sitting. I soon realized he was drunk again. How could he get so drunk again so quickly? I was about to leave when he asked me to stay, that he would be right back. He disappeared into another room and quickly returned with a handgun that he pointed right between my eyes. He said, 'this pistol has a hair trigger so don't move.' He then asked me to go into the kitchen and fix him a sandwich. I said, 'yes sir, just what kind of sandwich do you want?' He then came into the kitchen, stood close beside me, dropped his hand with the pistol and fired. I looked down and saw a bullet hole about one inch from my foot. He then handed me the pistol and I ran like hell.

This was one of my first introductions to ministry in the parish. It was enough to put my soft spot to sleep forever.

TO BE HEALED

How am I to be healed
with your feel good celebrations?
See my wounds
from which flows
the gift of God,
back again and again in the
brokenness that surrounds you.

HOME

Where families embrace
love abides and thrives
innocence and solitude shows itself sadly
community gathers
and warmly scatters,
leaving the homeless, homeless
single tears in a lake of gladness.
Home, yet not at home,
a part of, yet set apart.
Sweetness destroys the soul
leaving the tartness of life
that makes us sore.

Our families are where we first learn about ourselves. Our core identity comes first from the mirroring eyes of our primary caretakers. Our destiny depended to a large extent on the health of our caretakers.

John Bradshaw

CANDY

In every age and culture there appears to be that person who is held up as pure and innocent; the one who has childlike qualities that the community holds in great esteem and in which is often found God or Godlike attributes. Perhaps the need for such individuals is necessary for our projections – a place or container that can hold the goodness that we, ourselves, can't possibly, or don't want to, live up to. We find such an archetype in *Psyche* 1 who is ultimately sacrificed to the gods. We also find this in the Gospels when Jesus is referred to as "good teacher" and he quickly refutes this, saying, "Why do you call me good, no one is good but the Father." Jesus quickly rejected becoming an icon or container for goodness, knowing how he could be set up to carry or contain that which others need to claim within themselves or to place it where it belongs; only with God the Father. In modern times we have experienced a similar archetype in the person of Marilyn Monroe who became the projection of every American male. She was the goddess of sex and beauty, the all but perfect woman that men in our culture hold in great esteem, a woman of physical beauty and attraction; and yet, here is an icon, a woman who cannot possibly live up to such projections and whose life ends in tragedy. It is said that every male in America killed Marilyn Monroe. Projections are unconscious, and cannot be taken back, only reflected upon and hopefully learned from, however, this seems rarely to be the case. Making the unconscious conscious is a bit too frightening for most of us and we would just as soon let sleeping dogs lie, lest their bite becomes too painful. So we just stuff the unconscious with threatening thoughts casting a long dark shadow and remaining unaware of the light that forms such dark images in our lives. It would appear the further we get from the light the longer and darker our shadow becomes causing a dark image that stretches long and wide affecting many within its path, even for generations to come. The longer, darker and more frightening our shadow becomes the more it is screaming at us to take notice that we might become more the persons we were created to be in God's image. According to C.G. Jung this is the process of individualization.

Candy was fourteen when I first met her. She had a beautiful smile and knew it. It was most difficult not to be attracted to this child who warmed your heart and brought laughter to your soul. She was indeed sweet, just like her name "Candy" and people swarmed around her as flies on honey. I'm not sure of the origin of her name but whoever gave it to her did her no favor. People have a tendency to live up to their names even, and especially, to a fault. Candy was no exception, and in due time, "Candy" was destined to become "Bitter" and live out a tragic life. When I first came to Beattyville Candy was one of the first church members I met; It seemed she popped up most everywhere. I learned Candy was the youngest of three daughters of a mother who suffered from a mental illness and was in and out of the hospital. The father was alcoholic and a truck driver, a combination, which ordinarily doesn't mix well. The best I could tell he drank more than he drove. The two older daughters were around but didn't show themselves much, at least not to me. Candy appeared to have a strained relationship with her sisters. She didn't seem to get much from them and I wondered if they were not in the way for

Candy. I'm not sure what this meant except that this family was so dysfunctional that it was hard to figure out, except you knew it wasn't good. Candy had much anger that she covered up with her sweetness, that pleasant smile and the way in which she managed to win the hearts and souls of so many people. Candy desperately wanted a family, someone to love and to love her. Everything Candy did and said seemed to say, 'love me' and 'protect me'. For all practical reasons Candy was an orphan looking for a way home and yet she always seemed to look in the wrong places. Just perhaps Candy and Marilyn Monroe had much in common.

Members of the church who took an interest in her basically raised Candy. Or was it pity for this child, left to raise herself for the most part without parents? She attended church almost every Sunday and often came to special events, such as potluck dinners and the like. It was like Candy was community property. I'm not sure just how many families in the church had her eating and rooming in their homes but I know one in particular that took her in a great deal of the time. The father of this family was a teacher at the high school and the mother a sweet woman who gave herself totally to her children, three girls to be precise. Then of course Candy made it four girls since she was in this home so much. It was not until many years later that the middle daughter was telling me how much Candy resented their intact family and often wondered why she couldn't have such a family. It appears that Candy never got over her hurt and bitterness. As long as she was in high school she made the best of it and could always be seen at all the activities. She was a varsity cheerleader and enjoyed every minute of it.

Candy got frightened in her senior year of high school wondering just what she would do after graduation. I will always think this is why she got pregnant by one of the most no count boys in Beattyville. Jeff was into drugs big time and was in no way ready to be a husband and father. Candy burned all her bridges and went from being the town sweetheart to the town whore. It was as if she consciously set out to let everyone see and know what she really thought of herself, and was determined to live out her script; a script that seemed to say that she was not worthy of love and full acceptance by anyone. I often wondered what her relationship with her mother was during the first year of her life. It is a known fact that when the mother is inattentive, uncaring and uninterested in the infant, he or she grows into a child and adult whose sense of identity is seriously defective. It is during these early years that we learn who we are and who we are not. We develop a sense of "me" – my arm, my face, my thoughts, my voice, my family, and my feelings. It is in these early years that the world is viewed as either hostile or friendly and we begin learning that these limits are our boundaries. In the field of psychology the knowledge of these limits is what is meant by ego boundaries.

I saw Candy through her pregnancy and offered as much support as I could or knew how to offer. I felt extremely helpless. I thought if I felt this much helplessness Candy must feel even more helpless in the face of this situation. I was also angry, angry at the church for not being supportive of Candy, but rather withdrawing from her and having only negative thoughts, thoughts that were in no way helpful to Candy or for the church that should be an example of the living Christ in community.

Just before I left Beattyville, Candy came to me asking that I baptize her baby. I shared with her that baptism has three important meanings in the Presbyterian Church. Foremost it means that she wishes to reaffirm her faith and promises to raise her child in the church, seeing that the child attends worship and study, working toward a full understanding of what God has done for us in Jesus Christ. Second, it means we give this child unto God for God's blessings, knowing that in baptism she will be marked by Christ forever; and last, the congregation will be asked to help us to nurture and raise our children, to take spiritual responsibility by actively teaching, supporting and nurturing all baptized children in the congregation. This would be a big step for Candy considering how the members of the congregation were responding to her situation of having a child out of wedlock. It would also be a big step for the church to receive this baptism. After much discussion Candy insisted that this was what she wanted for her baby regardless of the tension that was present between her and the congregation.

On my last Sunday in Beattyville I approached the Session, which in the Presbyterian Church is the ruling body of officers called Elders, and shared with them that we would have a baptism during morning worship. I further stated that I expected them to offer their full support and to do all possible to live out the church's responsibilities regarding Candy and her baby. They were silent.

One of the greatest pleasures of my ministry was to be able to baptize Candy's baby in this congregation. To walk down the center aisle of the church, holding the baby in my arms, looking directly into the eyes of each member asking that they live up to their commitment to help Candy nurture this child in the ways of the Lord. What a wonderful way to depart as their pastor.

It has been a mystery to me why we respond the way we do to our environment, especially when it comes to our families of origin. Regardless of our position in the birth order, the financial status of the family and the ability or inability of our parents to provide a loving and protective environment, we are all looking for a way home. Henri Nouwen has drawn my attention to the story of the prodigal son (or is it the story of the loving father?), in juxtaposition to Rembrandt's painting of the Return of the Prodigal Son.2 It's heart warming to see this youngest son in rags with his left sandal off and exposing a bare foot with cuts and bruises acquired from the journey home, kneeling before his father. It brings tears to the eyes seeing this father holding his son with obvious compassion and celebration. There stands the oldest in his finest clothes and jewelry standing tall and smug, a son who has never left home and yet remains homeless. Probably most of us take up for and identify with this oldest son who feels he has done no wrong, and has little mercy for anyone who lacks responsibility for themselves.

When you have begun with no home I guess it's an especially difficult journey to find your way home. When your father was never there for you, I suspect it would be hard to imagine a father waiting on the road for your return; a father that would embrace you and even give a party in your name. It has been said that we perceive our heavenly father much in the same manner as we experience our earthly father. I have often thought of Candy in this regard, as one who would like more than anything to be at home, but just can't seem to get there. Many of us spend most of our lives trying to get home but continually run into barriers that work against even beginning the journey, while others of us stay at home, yet never experience being at home. What a contrast between these two spiritually frustrating positions of life, archetypes that all of us know too well.

I guess I had been away from Beattyville about ten years when I received a call from Candy. I was in Savannah, Georgia, and Candy was the last person from whom I expected to hear. Native Eastern Kentuckians rarely ventured very far away from home and even to call someone as far away as Savannah was just unheard of. A trip to Lexington, which was less than a hundred miles away, could be traumatic let alone traveling to Savannah, Georgia, or even to entertain the idea, was just not something a person in this part of the country would do.

Candy's call reminded me of another call I had received from Ms. Zora, an Elder in the Saint Helen's Church, asking if I would drive a woman to Lexington. Wanda was pregnant with her sixth child and was told if she carried the baby it could easily take her life. Wanda agreed, after much persuasion, to being admitted into a hospital in Lexington for termination of the pregnancy. The trip was pleasant enough with Wanda remaining mostly silent, which I felt demonstrated her anxious state. This was a tremendous step for Wanda since her children were all she had. Wanda was a poor and uneducated woman who lived with her mother in an unpainted run-down house up the hollow from off the Jackson Road. As well as I remember she had never been married and lived pretty much an isolated life. I helped Wanda get checked into the hospital staying with her through the whole admitting process. I did not leave to return to Beattyville until I saw Wanda in bed in her room. Wanda appeared to be o.k. with this whole process, not totally accepting and certainly not comfortable, but o.k.

When I returned home I got a call from Mrs. Zora who told me that Wanda had beaten me home. To this day I don't know how she did it! This only reinforced with me how difficult it is for people in Appalachia to leave their comfortable surroundings regardless of the circumstances.

I had first hand experience with folk in Eastern Kentucky who found it so hard to leave home. Wanda just wasn't at home in that Lexington hospital and there was no way she was going to stay. Yet as I think upon Candy's journey to visit me in Savannah I began to understand increasingly that Candy just wasn't at home anywhere. Candy most likely could identify equally with either the youngest or the oldest son in the parable, in that like the oldest she could be at home doing all the right things and yet never feeling at home, never feeling the love she had always sought after and that all of us need if we are to be fully human, a feeling of being at home, accepted and loved for just who you are. Candy could just as easily identify with the youngest son, tired and dirty and wanting to return home even if it meant being a hired servant. Where is this home? Who would welcome her? Who was waiting and watching for her? Who would embrace her? Who would give her a party and celebrate her return? I anxiously waited for Candy 's arrival as a father would for a long lost daughter. We spent hours talking sometimes into the late night; at other times taking long walks on the beach in our bare feet with the gentle roaring waves moving in and over our ankles and providing rest for our souls.

Candy was questioning her life. Why doesn't my sister believe me? Why do I have a husband that is away from home more than he is at home? Why do others have responsible families and my family is so chaotic, so wounded and disengaging? Isn't it interesting how we repeat our family of origin unless we consciously work toward making it different and even then it is often difficult to achieve. I have a special place in my heart for Candy and I only wish I could answer all her questions and make her happy, but this is way beyond me, and I suspect anyone's, ability.

We are all on a journey home, that place where we are accepted and loved for just who we are rather than a product of our parents, a particular school of thought or shaped by our friends who reward us for being a particular way or exhibiting a behavior pleasing to others. Some of us come from loving families that give us more to work with than others. I was most fortunate to have loving parents and in particular a loving father who accepted me for who I was. I have shared this with others who respond, "You are so fortunate." This tells me that most of us are not so fortunate and that many have a difficult road to travel to arrive home, given the home life from which they have come.

According to Webster the very first definitions of home is 'hide' "to lie down" and 'rest.' This might remind us of a place of security, a place where we get away from the busy, stressful and often dysfunctional world we live in. We often hear the statement "home sweet home" which might be referred to as a place of peace, rest and quietness at the end of a long journey. People of faith frequently speak of home as more than a place, but rather a state of living in grace, which God, alone can give. Is this not what the youngest son came to realize on his long walk home, or Dorothy after arriving in Oz? There is no place like home. This kind of home can't be built, or bought or caused by some kind of magic or science, but only through faith in God. We all work so hard building a place where we can "hide" or seek security through the material, which is necessary, but will always leave us short of real peace or home that the youngest son finally sought in his Father. We often mistake the oldest son as being at home but he is the farthest away from home and doesn't know it.

Jesus was a master at telling parables and in the Gospel of Luke we find the parable of Lazarus and the Rich Man.

"There was a rich man, and he was clothed in purple and fine linen and feasted sumptuously day by day. And at his gate a poor man named Lazarus was laid, full of sores, who desired to be fed with what fell from the rich man's table; moreover, the dogs came and licked his sores. The poor man died and was carried by the angels to Abraham's bosom. The rich man died also, and he was buried; and in Hades, being in torment, he lifted up his eyes and saw Abraham far off and Lazarus in his bosom.

And he called out, 'Father Abraham, have mercy on me, and send Lazarus to dip the end of his finger in water and cool my tongue; for I am in anguish in this flame.' But Abraham said, 'Son, remember that you in your lifetime received your good things, and Lazarus in like manner bad things; but now he is comforted here, and you are in anguish. And besides all this, between us and you, a great chasm has been fixed, in order that those who would pass from here to you may not be able, and no one may cross from there to us.'" And he said, 'Then I beg you, father, to send him to my father's house, for I have five brothers, in order that he may warn them, lest they also come into this place of torment.' "But Abraham said, they have Moses and the prophets; let them hear them.' "And he said, 'No father Abraham; but if someone goes to them from the dead, they will repent.' He said to him, 'If they do not

71

hear Moses and the prophets, neither will they be convinced if someone should rise from the dead.

Luke 16:19-31

Many of Jesus' parables speak of the necessity of including the inferior element. John A. Sanford in his book *The Kingdom Within* suggests this parable be given an inward interpretation seeing the rich man as the ego, "... which has everything its own way and falls prey to a hubris so that it unfairly dominates the entire psyche. The poor man, Lazarus, is the rejected one; a personality shoved by the ego into the unconscious but is denied it."3 I think this is one important reason I often think of "Candy" – she, and many others like her, hold me responsible to my unconscious, which I would just as soon forget. "Candy" in many ways represents or carries all that which I prefer not to look at my own sense of 'homelessness', my own feelings of rejection, my own loneliness and displacement. Sanford continues to comment on this parable by saying, "The 'inferior personality' – that is, Lazarus in the story – is, ...elevated by God. The story shows that what people have regarded as inferior, unworthy, and to be scorned is favored, loved, and elevated by God."4

When I think of the wonderful home consisting of a loving mother and father with three beautiful daughters, of which "Candy" was so much a part, I think of C.J. Jung's concept of the number four symbolizing wholeness. Just perhaps "Candy" was the fourth girl that brought about a sense of wholeness or balance. The acceptance rather than rejection of "Candy" just might have made possible the nourishment of the soul for all parties. Just perhaps Candy represents the dark side of many of us, that side, which we would rather not consider but quickly reject. Yet as long as we reject this darkness, or better yet, that which we perceive as darkness, the more we live in an illusion and will never benefit from the blessings of disillusionment.

I recently returned to this small Kentucky town where I

had a pastorate. As I entered town many memories flooded my mind and it was hard to believe it had been so many years ago. Of course the town had made some changes and I had to take a second look to familiarize myself with the new look that had eliminated some landmarks. I always remembered coming into the town from a steep decline with my favorite restaurant lying at the bottom of this hill on the corner of Main Street. The steep decline had been widened and straightened out in such a manner that it didn't seem like the same place. I was disheartened to hear how a runaway truck had crashed into the restaurant and completely destroyed it. That restaurant had the best pies I think I had ever eaten. And then there was the church I had served setting right beside where the restaurant had been. The church must have come close to being destroyed as well.

I drove to the house of one of the Elders but found that he was not at home. But while preparing to back out of his drive he and his wife pulled in. It was a joy to visit even for a few minutes. Of course his children, like mine, had all grown, married and left home. Things change except for the memories and the stories we had to share.

I then drove over to Candy's house. I could not return to this village without trying to visit Candy. I pulled up into her drive. Dogs barked and cats scattered as heads rose from those sitting in the yard. I got out and Candy immediately came and gave me a big hug. Candy said, "They all wondered who in the world was coming up the drive. And I said, 'That's Tom.' That was a good feeling. Not only being remembered but also feeling at home. Candy acted as if it was only yesterday that I was there as her pastor.

Seeing and visiting with Candy that day brought various feelings and memories to mind, some good, others painful but to know Candy to be happy and at home with her family gave me great pleasure.

THE WARMTH OF A HUG

The warmth of a hug,
folding into the arms of another,
seeking lost security
if only for the moment.

Hugs turn cold when not at home,
fire burns in another,
while the journey continues
on the cold open road.

Oh to return home,
to a home that never existed,
who stands waiting
for the traveling one?

Embracing the memories,
Knowing we are at rest,
seeing promise even in darkness
brings brightness, a joy to the soul.

HANNAH

Hannah was cooking soup in a pressure cooker on the stove in her kitchen. The burner was going strong as if to say, go! go! The lid was on tight with a rubber gasket, which seemed to say, no! no! Between the go! go! and the no! no! was that which was trying to find just the right place for a good bowl of soup. Hannah got anxious and pulled off the lid completely destroying her kitchen and ended up in the hospital with third degree burns over half of her body. Too bad she couldn't have used the steam release valve on the lid to relieve the pressure.

Man's whole history consists from the beginning in a conflict between his feelings of inferiority and his arrogance.

C.G. Jung

What gives soul to people is the capacity to experience the paradox of life.

Greek psychologist
Evangelos Christou

THE PURPLE DUSTER

I answered the phone and a familiar voice said, "Hi Tom, this is Alice, how is everything in Kentucky?" It was good to hear from an old friend in Michigan and to know I wasn't forgotten. Things hadn't changed much with the church that continued to be divided over various issues. Then there was the womanizing egocentric preacher terrorizing the women of the church with his arrogant grin and inappropriate invitation to get them alone with him as the occasion arose. I got an earful before Alice really told me what she had called about. Alice knew a young woman who had just finished her student teaching and had hoped to teach in Kentucky. Just perhaps, she thought, I could manage to get this young woman a job, being that I was the preacher of the Presbyterian Church. It was not at all unusual for Presbyterians to have leadership positions in the community and often to be the ones with the most education. Presbyterians take much pride in their educational institutions and even more pride in their members who hold high degrees in various professional fields, education being one of many. I assured Alice I would do what I could and asked that she give my love to the folks in Bay City.

In 1921 and 1922 my Dad attended Kentucky Normal College in Louisa, Kentucky during the winter months, which allowed him to take and pass a state examination awarding him a second-class elementary certificate. My Dad had started out as a young man teaching in rural Kentucky, a part of Appalachia that snuggled up really close to West Virginia, with one room county school houses known as Clifford, Baker's Gap and Upper Tug. Dad would often tell stories of his teaching experience.

> I had a cousin, William Frazier, who was apparently jealous of me. One afternoon, he stood up at his desk and threw a rock that hit the blackboard beside me. He threw a rock at me in school! I went back and just collared him and brought him up front and beat the devil out of him with a big stick. I kept a baseball bat in my desk drawer the rest of that term of school. On top of that, the Superintendent of schools came up there and I had to stand trial. It had a big attendance. The house was crowded. Everybody was there! I told them my story. They told the Superintendent his story. The Superintendent said: "It's alright. Just forget about it."…. And dismissed it.

My brother commented, saying, "In those days not much effort was wasted on the niceties. People, especially school teachers, related to people in a straightforward and no-nonsense sort of way."

I wondered what might be in store for our new school teacher. I was so instrumental in bringing her to the community and, even more important, what might be in store for the community? Can a young woman just out of college in Michigan find a place for herself in the hills of Eastern Kentucky?

A Purple Duster pulled off the highway into the drive without any hesitation, just as if it knew where it was going. Out jumped a young woman who identified herself as Sally

Hayes. I knew I was going to enjoy Sally the moment I saw her big smile and the very way in which she carried herself; a body language that expressed a sense of freedom, warmth and acceptance. With our family, she fit and wore extremely well, like a frequently used chair that everyone fought over because of its comfort; a chair that wasn't especially attractive and yet discarding of it was not an option. We all loved Sally, especially the children, and knew she would make a wonderfully exciting elementary teacher. It was hard to imagine how any child could not love and enjoy Sally. She was full of stories which our children loved to hear and not only was she good at sharing stories, she was equally as good at listening with great interest and enthusiasm; a balance infrequently experienced in people, and which needs to be utilized and rewarded in any community that values education.

Sally was young and eager to begin her teaching career. I had gotten her in touch with Henry Sebastian who was superintendent at the Lee County School System. Henry was a prince of a man and highly thought of and respected by everyone. Of all the folk of Lee County Henry and his wife probably had the most 'class'. They were members of the Presbyterian Church and lived in a beautiful two-story house just outside of town on the Booneville Highway. The Sebastian place was spacious with many acres of rolling hills and could be seen from our living room window. Much of this estate was now overcome with kudzu that sometimes had to be trimmed away from the highway. I often thought kudzu could be a strong Christian symbol, even more so than holly or evergreen, in that it is green to represent eternal life and it is very strong. People in the southern states have been trying to get rid of this fast growing vine for years but it just won't die. Kudzu spreads, as Christians should spread the good news, but there is a downside in that it smothers and kills everything with which it comes in contact; but perhaps everything has its dark side, which provides a sense of balance and even wholeness of life. However, most would see this imported erosion buster as the work of the devil long before they could even imagine it being a sign or symbol for Christ and his church. Unlike the kudzu that was overtaking the countryside, Henry Sebastian was a man to whom both Sally and I were indebted for making it possible for Sally to begin her teaching career in the Appalachian foothills of Lee County.

Not only was Henry Sebastian helpful in securing a teaching job for Sally but also was extremely sensitive toward my son. Henry had a perfect view of our driveway and could see Mark playing basketball without a hoop or backboard. Mark had a circle drawn above the garage door and would throw the ball and make believe he had a real hoop. It wasn't long before Henry had a beautiful steel freestanding basketball goal constructed at the Vocational School. Not only did Henry have it made but also erected beside the drive in the back of the garage, which made an ideal place for a basketball goal. Mark was the envy of every boy in the county. I guess being a preacher's son has some perks.

Where Sally was a delight for us she became a pain and real source of frustration for others. Sally had a lot in common with kudzu in this regard. I guess it all started when she rented an apartment from Aunt Lou who ran the only motel in the county. Aunt Lou was up in years and had an apartment for rent on the basement level of her house, which was next door to the motel. The apartment was only half submerged into the ground in that the entrance was from the ground level off the back yard. Aunt Lou needed someone to fill that space so she wouldn't feel so alone, moreover to feel more secure knowing someone was there and could be called upon in case of an emergency. Sally felt good about the apartment. The space was just right and the rent was something she could afford so Aunt Lou and Cathy made a deal which both were soon to regret.

On top of Spencer's ridge abandoned farms could be

seen running along the narrow valley of the middle fork of the Kentucky River. It had been a number of years since anyone took any interest in this land where weeds and saplings snarled and twisted their way through old farmhouses, privies and barns, across abandoned roads and throughout this rich bottom land. Who could imagine anyone farming this land again! Most would rather live in poverty and let the government provide through welfare checks which was exactly what most in Lee County were prone to do; just have many babies and look to the 'give-er-ment.' However, if it were not for government money as welfare checks this community would not only be depressed, it would be dead.

The sixties were confusing and often turbulent for many, especially those under thirty who were fast raising our consciousness so that we could not help but look at important issues of our day. The Vietnam War was winding down but not without many feelings toward our country and the revolution that had reshaped its attitudes and values; some for the good and others not so good, according to one's political, social and spiritual views. Many disillusioned college students dropped out of school forming counter cultures based upon simple life styles, which were reminiscent of early pioneers, who lived in small settlements and grubbed out their sustenance from the earth.

It was just such a group of young people who had bought a farm on the river and literally cleared the land with axes and shovels to plant crops and raise a few cows, pigs and chickens. It was a sight to see this land come to life again with energy and enthusiasm from a handful of University of Kentucky dropouts. However, some saw them as dregs of society, draft dodgers and hippies that only continued to embarrass the county with their long hair, shabby clothes and bandannas, the revolutionary uniform of the day. Others admired their ingenuity, creativity and hard work that they had invested into a land that had long been forsaken and forgotten. Sally found herself enjoying these folk at the commune in that they were about her age and talked the same political and social language. There was one particular man that Sally took a liking to and soon the feeling became mutual and they began seeing much of each other. Sally was spending increasing time at the commune, leaving a strip of purple down the highway each day after school as she headed toward Spencer's Ridge.

One Saturday evening Sally invited all the members of the commune to her apartment for a picnic in the back yard. There was much loud music, beer drinking, and pot smoking while the grills slowly cooked ribs saturated in barbecue sauce. The more beer they drank the louder they got until you could hear them out on the highway. Sophia had just returned from visiting relatives in Pennsylvania and had brought back some beautiful loaves of Greek bread braided like a show horse's tail. You would have thought it was some Greek love feast as they danced and fell all over each other, but it was only a small group of young adults with raging hormones out to have a little fun. However, Aunt Lou didn't see any humor in any of these activities and come Monday morning she was going to see that this woman was thrown out of her apartment and, if possible, out of the county.

By noon on Monday Sally was the talk of the town. The lovely school teacher from Michigan had become little more than the whore who was brought in by the Presbyterian preacher. It was bad enough for Sally to have a beer drinking party but to have it at her apartment with the members of the commune was just too much for this small town. The telephone lines were hot and the more the people talked the more exaggerated it became. There was nothing I could do. Sally had dug a hole too deep for anyone to get her out of. Sally resigned her teaching position and moved in with the folk at the commune, which just further reinforced the people's notion that this young woman was no good and they gloried in her good riddance. We didn't see much of Sally after this except for an occasional flash of purple down Booneville Highway in front of the house. I could only smile and wish her well as one of God's children looking for her place and purpose in life and doing so in an innocent and foolish manner.

Kudzu was imported from the orient to prevent soil erosion and could not be a better paradox for Sally and the Appalachia in which she lived for this brief time in her life. Paradoxically Sally was a rich gift bringing joy to many while angering and alienating others. Just like kudzu she does her job but not without the expense of inconvenience. As summer brings warmth and new growth so winter brings cold dark days that can weight us down heavily. Sally cannot be thought of without addressing the paradox of life in general and just perhaps nothing has real meaning or importance apart from paradox that nurtures our soul. I suspect we are all seeking a higher awareness of who we are and what it means to be fully human. I know of no one book or person filled with precise instructions on how to be fully human, to be the persons God has intended us to be. Such a statement might appall many conservative Christians and yet if we think about it Christianity is a journey toward wholeness, a process filled with paradox that often spins us first one way and then another. Spiritual wholeness is a process, a journey or quest that has many ups and downs, first twisting us one way and then another lending to much confusion. Paul says it well in his letter to the Romans, "I do not understand my own actions. For I do not do what I want, but I do the very thing I hate." (Romans 14:15.) This is no different than our first story, our genesis, our beginning that is so well told in the Hebrew Scriptures; the story that tells us so well how we gained our humanity; the story that reminds us of who we are and our inability to be anything other than human, sinful, fragile and constantly struggling with this inner conflict of being both human (flesh) and divine (breathing the very breath of God). Life is a divine/human drama that has been fulfilled in the person of Jesus yet still leaves us with our own struggle that Paul alludes to when he says, "...work out your own salvation with fear and trembling." (Philippians 2:12)

There are two accounts of the creation of man. According to Genesis 2:7, "Yahweh God fashioned man of the dust from the soil. Then he breathed into his nostril a breath of life, and thus man became a living being. Man *(adam)* comes from earth *(adamah)* and shall return to it. (Genesis 3:19,23) Man is thus a union of opposites, matter and spirit, but with an emphasis on matter since his very name means earth. This same idea is expressed another way in the other account. "God created man in the image of himself, in the image of God he created him, male and female he created them." (Genesis 1:27) The God-image lodged in a creature of earth corresponds to the union of spirit and matter. 1

During my ministry I have come to understand this creation story as a story of our coming into our own or a grounding process accompanying conscious realization. Another way of saying the same thing is that this story is about "falling upward" rather than its typical interpretation of a fall from grace. The paradox of falling upward embraces the awkwardness of this whole story, which seeks to explain in mythological fashion how we came to be uniquely human in communion with God and our fellow human beings. It is important that we not misinterpret the concept of myth in this rich story.

A myth, for most of us, means something that is illusory, foolish or false. This view of myth comes from our ignorance about the meaning of mythology, and is most unfortunate, for a myth is a particular form of story that conveys powerful psychological and spiritual truths. Myths are to the human race, as a whole, as dreams are to the individual: pictorial representations of what is taking place in the Soul. 2

Can you imagine staying in the garden as God created it and us? We would be little more than puppets animated only by the pulling of strings by the hands of God. The rich soul that first told this story had a wonderful imagination into our human nature and the creative aspects of a loving humanistic

God. What kind of life would we have without sin and guilt and the loving aspects of God?

This wonderful garden story has many implications for our lives; but how might it fit into Sally's experience in Eastern Kentucky? Was she invited into a garden as innocent, unaware of her own nakedness? Had she not studied diligently until she got her degree in elementary education and now looking to expand her life, to look beyond the books and to explore life more fully? Oh, like most of us in similar situations, she was not conscious of such need and the trek she was about to take, leading her to encounter the serpent, biting the apple and blaming Eve.

> Eve bites into the fruit. Suddenly she realizes that she is naked. She begins to cry. The kindly serpent picks up a handkerchief, gives it to her. "It's all right," he says. "The first moment is always the hardest." "But I thought knowledge would be so wonderful," Eve says, sniffing. "Knowledge?!" laughs the serpent. "This fruit is from the Tree of *Life*."

> *In the Garden*, by Stephen Mitchell

Certain Gnostic sects would see the serpent as the spiritual redeemer of man and God as the evil demiurge.

Indeed it does appear that God only wishes to dominate and control as a feudal lord where the serpent offers to them a conscious life with open eyes. Such consciousness is painful, as they have to realize their sexuality, becoming shy about their bodies as they sew together fig leaves for clothing. When sin is discovered pain is realized as in childbirth; weeding must take place if food is to be grown for we have been driven out of the garden with an angel at the gate holding a flaming sword that we might never reenter. (Genesis 3:24)

This God of the garden story has a lot in common with the God that cut a deal over Job. What kind of God would enter into a bet with Satan – a bet in which Satan said he could take over Job's soul by having Job become unfaithful toward God and instead faithful to Satan? What kind of God would use his servant as a pawn to win a bet? To make things worse not to be willing to talk about this whole episode with Job once God became the winner (so to speak); perhaps a God who would place a serpent in the garden only to predict the "fall" of his prized creation of man and woman. According to C.G. Jung in his wonderful little book entitled *Answer to Job* we find that God had no desire to talk with Job about this matter but only became defensive, saying, "Who is this that darkens counsel by words without insight?" (Job 38:2)

> ...it is Yahweh himself who darkens his own counsel and who has no insight. He turns the tables on Job and blames him for what he does himself: man is not permitted to have an opinion about him, and, in particular, is to have no insight which he himself does not possess. 3

What is Job's guilt other than wanting an explanation? Job wanted only to talk with God and learn about the ways of God and his own pain, suffering and faithfulness. God would have nothing of it. What is Adam and Eve's guilt other than wanting to be real, to be conscious and fully human? The implications of all this goes much further than these rich stories of the Old Testament or the story of Sally in her purple duster. When injustice is experienced by anyone from those in power it is often futile to receive a hearing or receive justice because ultimate power is unable to reflect upon them to gain the amount of consciousness necessary for justice. Therefore violence is often the result leaving the afflicted with only their higher sense of consciousness based on self-reflection and deep faith.

> But what does man possess that God does not have? Because of his littleness, puniness, and defenselessness against the Almighty, he possesses..., a somewhat keener consciousness based on self-reflection: he must, to survive, always be mindful of his impotence. 4

I feel certain that C.G. Jung came to these conclusions because of his experience with his father who was a rigid reformed Swiss cleric. When Carl was exploring the faith he often questioned his father who would respond, "Oh nonsense, you always want to think. One ought not think, but believe". 5 Is it no wonder that Jung was in defense of Job and Adam and Eve? In Jung's evening of life he was asked if he believed in God and he answered that he didn't believe in God he *knew* there was a God. I have often heard it said that the way we see our earthly father is often the way we see God.

> The major threats to our survival no longer stem from nature without but from our own nature within. It is our carelessness, our hostilities, our selfishness and pride and willful ignorance that endanger the world. Unless we can now tame and transmute the potential for evil in the human soul, we shall be lost. 6

I read this quote by Scott Peck in the introduction of Matthew Fox's book *Sins of The Spirit, Blessings of the Flesh*, while it was still hot off the press with our country in shock and deep depression following 9/11. It is easy to become unnecessarily defensive, strike out at weak nations (Iraq) while failing to take seriously our own evil involvement in the world. This is not to dismiss the evil of terrorism in the world but rather to become more conscious of our own evil. Saint Augustine once stated, "Never fight evil if it is totally outside of yourself". The primitive idea of God in both the garden story and in Job demonstrates that even God has a dark side about which he gets defensive and only wants to use power to engage his people rather than to relate on a more conscious level. The purple duster runs the roads even today, kudzu continues to win the battle in the hill country of the South and "hippies" build communities, which most distinctively thrive outside the garden walls.

There is no better contemporary illustration of our need to jump the garden wall than the movie entitled *Mona Lisa Smile*.7 Here Julia Roberts plays an art history professor (Katherine Watson) at an all girls "finishing school" where she finds the students brilliant yet trapped behind walls of traditionalism and authoritarianism that prevents them from becoming whole persons. This movie demonstrates how far we have come since the 1950s, allowing students and women, in particular, the freedom of original thought.

> The search for spirit, for God, is ultimately the quest to know ourselves in our heights and depths. It is the task of every man and woman and of every heroic journey to go beyond our certitudes and doubts, beyond our sure know-ledge and understanding, in the direction of an ever-unfolding truth. It was, is, and always will be the greatest human adventure...8

The search for spirit, or God, was the quest of the first man and woman and has been our quest ever since. When we see the purple duster running the highways we see a person who has 'fallen upward,' one who has escaped from the garden and knows what it's like to be fully human. Not to be fully human is to remain in a box, contained, restrained and extremely limited to explore oneself or God more fully. Being cast out of the garden is to be recognized as human rather than a puppet on strings which God alone controls. Once we deal with our shame and guilt responsibly and accept our free will we can then and only then begin our spiritual journey knowing that we are both human and divine. We can now more fully know that we are flesh made of the earth and spirit, God's breath that animates us giving us the life we have always wanted but could not claim until we left our original home. It is only by leaving home that we can gain this balance, this sense of wholeness with the full capacity for holiness.

The Appalachian people in many ways are both cursed and blessed by their garden, a garden of beautiful mountains and a strong identity to a culture that defines them through language, arts and ancestry; a garden that holds them unnecessarily to a land that is restrictive, unproductive, raped and abused. Many of the mountain people are confined to this geographic area of the country through family loyalty, which prevents them from moving beyond the county in which they were born. Both a feeling of insecurity and fear prevails that keeps many from moving beyond these garden walls. Perhaps rather than religious snake handlers they need a wise serpent to encourage them to move beyond the garden wall and seek to be more whole persons. Can we stay behind our walls of comfort where almost everything is defined and provided for us and be genuinely human and divine?

My brother Jim (the family historian), told me a story about our father, who was the oldest of nine children from a poor family in Lawrence County. It appears that in some context dad's sister, and our Aunt Dorie, told that dad never went to church with the family on Sunday but would always be seen reading something under a big tree. Dad was also the only one of the nine that left Lawrence County, for an education at the Roanoke Business College. My brother further told me that when he was accepted into this school that he did not have the money to travel to Roanoke but made it only by the grace of a relative who was willing to give him a loan.

My father wanted more. He was not satisfied with the simple, naïve life in the hills of Lawrence County. He was not satisfied with the fundamentalist Christian faith that was filled with much emotionalism; but rather sought to be stretched in body, mind and soul.

Did he listen to the serpent? Perhaps. Or was it God? Sometimes it's difficult to tell the difference. Whatever it was allowed Dad to journey, gaining a higher sense of consciousness and developing a strong faith in God and himself that was passed on to his two sons.

There are many different garden walls but they all have the same effect on us. We can hide behind academics, ancestry, patriotism, religion or a number of institutions that will take us in and make us feel comfortable but at what cost? Such institutions will only instill guilt in us if we bite the apple and yet we know it's unavoidable unless we just want to be a kept people. The paradox is that we are both human and divine, made in God's image, and called to be the sons and daughters of God outside the garden wall, free to be the people we were created to be with unlimited potential.

> Then the Lord God said, see, the man has become like one of us, knowing good and evil; and now, he might reach out his hand and take also from the tree of life, and eat, and live forever.

Genesis 3:22

John A. Sanford helps us to see how the garden story is about wholeness.

> The Garden of Eden is a mandala, because of its central point with the remarkable trees, and the river flowing from it. A mandala is a concentric design that represents or symbolizes wholeness. In a mandala everything is grouped around a center. The shape of the mandala is circular, or, sometimes square. In a circle, every point on the circumference is equidistant from the center, so the shape of the circle suggests balance and completeness. Mandalas are represented in religious art all over the world. Many Christian churches, for instance, have mandalas in the form of the so-called Rose Windows of circular design. Because of the mandala shape of the garden, we are met immediately with the suggestion that the story is about wholeness – how man was originally contained within it, but then fell away from it. 9

A FALL INTO GRACE

Within the beautiful mandala
Potential to be
Curiosity, desire
To know power
Oh to be like God

Within the beautiful mandala
Seeking lost completeness
Yearning for wholeness
Man, woman – the urge to eat
To push upon the wall – to expand the mandala

Stretching out
Picking, eating
Freedom of choice
A gift of consciousness

Within the beautiful mandala
Lies birth, pain, guilt and nakedness
Hide! God comes in the cool of the evening
Walking in shadows
The dark side of God

Emerging from the beautiful mandala
Falling upward into our own
But not alone
Sojourning
A rendezvous with God

Within the beautiful mandala
A fall into grace
A gift of God

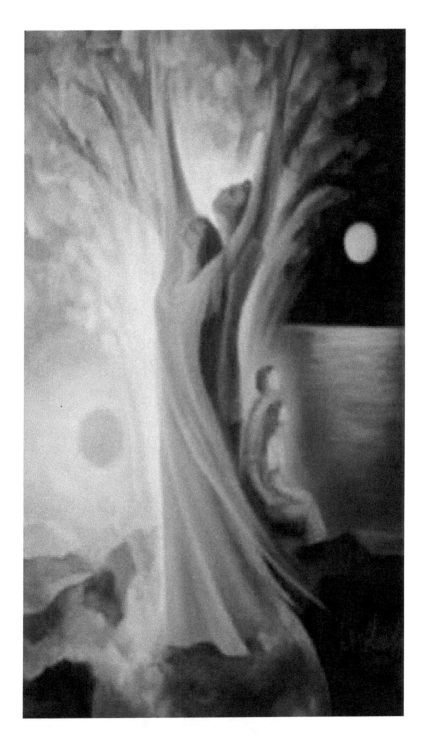

COMMUNITY

Fields lie dormant
with memories forgotten,
hopelessness breeds contempt
young minds question
as hearts beat silently
with blood running hot
and souls collaborate.

To hold in common
while privation separates,
communion a sham,
I don't know who I am
private or public,
sameness or diversity,
profane or holiness,
all look the same.

We are called into being by a God who uses communities to form us, and who uses communities to pull us back together when we have torn ourselves apart; but we have lost confidence in the communities we know best. ...and it is from that dilemma that God seeks to heal us.

Brian W. Grant

Community is not the only place where healing occurs, it is a means through which it happens.

Margaret Kornfeld

THE COMMUNE

Through Sally our family was able to establish a relationship with the people at the commune or what was commonly referred to as the 'hippy people.' Mark and Martha loved to visit and help them make corn meal and see the creative ways they had turned a dilapidated farmhouse and barn into living space. In the side of a small barn they had placed bottles of various colors, which let in light and provided a type of psychedelic effect inside the dwelling. This was a building meant for animals that was creatively made into a comfortable dwelling for people. Inside was a large room with a crude ladder leading up into the loft. It was in this loft that a young couple had placed an old bed, making it into their bedroom. From the outside it looked really no different from a barn except for the glass bottles and yet inside was a rather comfortable home with a unique primitive twist providing the essentials for house keeping. I personally found it most inviting in a type of romantic way, yet when I began seeing all the hard work that was involved in keeping up this commune I quickly changed my views. However, this newly decorated barn could easily be the envy of any young antiestablishment college age person during the sixties and early seventies. This community held all the symbols necessary to royally piss off any pro-establishment parent who found this community disgusting and even communistic in their life style and political views. Yet the members of this community had moved beyond the protest against Vietnam and other social concerns to a retreat back into the hills of Eastern Kentucky. These folk were out to reestablish themselves into a community designed and shaped by their own hands and minds, rather than to conform to a society that held few of their values or political views. The present society from which they had withdrawn was not to be trusted. Their votes didn't count, the God of the church was alien to their beliefs and Washington was dripping with the blood of too many innocent people. In many ways these young people had been defeated by the establishment and they were retreating to what they hoped would be a better world.

We could only visit when the weather permitted in that the road into the commune was unpaved and impassable during times of heavy rain or snow. The commune had a large four wheel drive truck, which was the only way they could get in and out in difficult times of the year. Just like the early pioneers these folk had left an unjust society ruled by kings of a sort and now were carving out their own place in the world, a place of hard work and family values that would reflect their view of a just and peaceable society.

The idealism and naivete of groups of this type too soon caught up with them. Such communities were full of novelty, built on a common faith, and filled with noble and just ideals of peace and justice for all. It did my heart good to experience a community built on such high expectations, and especially on the love they felt for one another and the collective drive to have a life based on principles different from the dominate society they had protested and from which they had withdrawn. Who can continue living in such primitive arrangements? Who can do without, when all around you see prosperity? Who can share and share alike treating one another as equals? Not even the early Christians could live in such an ideal community. What made these young people think they were any different? Who wants to be pregnant and so far away from a hospital? It was bad enough living in Beattyville with the closest hospital almost a hundred miles away, let alone living on an abandoned farm with limited transportation and an often-inaccessible road!

Most of these folk did not make it down on the farm but found themselves right back in the society against which they were protesting. It's hard to believe that these "hippies" assimilated back into the society from which they came; a society that fought in Vietnam, a society that to this day often remains indifferent to the needs of those unlike themselves. Malvina Reynolds wrote (Little Boxes, 1962) and sang of this era that included the words, "...those who live in houses of ticky-tack and all in a row." Now these people are in their fifties and sixties often referred to as 'yuppies'. Many have become successful in business and are enjoying the wealth that has come with the 1980s and 90s, an age that is often referred to as 'the age of selfishness'. What a change from the life and values they held to when they were down on the commune! There is one important difference with these "yuppies"; they don't trust anyone, especially institutions.

This lack of trust and inability to make commitments is the mark of the "yuppie" even today, perhaps especially today. I have a minister friend in the greater Atlanta area who has started a new church in the suburbs who doesn't dare ask his members to tithe or pledge a percentage to the church. Rather he has what he calls 'estimated giving', a stewardship program which requests no more than for each individual to write down what he/she thinks they will be giving to the church during the year. It is the total of these "estimated givings" that makes up the church's budget, and it is my understanding they always get more than what was estimated. My friend was smart to take so seriously the "yuppies" that makes up the majority of this congregation. These "yuppies" are now in their sixties and many in high salaried jobs. They have fared well in such an affluent society, a society built on such a strong military with corruption of every type. They took their stand during the days of the civil rights movement and Vietnam – from antiestablishment to the epitome of establishment; from down on the farm to high-styling city living where they have learned so well how to strive and thrive in a country that lives basically off the misfortunes of others around the world. What a contrast from the "hippie" movement of the sixties!

I like to look back on the days of the commune and to the political and social views they held. It always did my heart good to see their reaction to what I also saw as an evil society, even though I knew this scenario would not last, and that it was only a dream for the most part. The prophets of the day warmed my heart and gave me hope as I marched with Martin Luther King, Jr., with tears in my eyes and a song in my heart; marching in protest to the evils of the Vietnam War even, and perhaps especially, while members of the establishment cursed and spat upon us. Such experiences I hold dear to my heart, experiences that took place for the most part while I was attending Louisville Presbyterian Theological Seminary. These are some of the Kentucky heartstrings that continue to pull at me as if it were God or one of his angels continuing to get my attention. Many will tell me it was only the devil but I know the difference.

Where are the prophets today? Is this a dry period not unlike the times of Eli where we read in First Samuel "...the word of the Lord was rare..." or, are we in a time of prosperity such as the people of Israel and Judea just before they were taken into captivity to Babylon and Assyria? Perhaps we are in exile of a sort and don't know it. I keep looking for a prophet like Micah who was prophesying to a people like us in a country much like the United States:

> He has shown you, O man, what is good; and what does the Lord require of you but to do justice, and to love kindness, and to walk humbly with your God.

Micah 6:8

I had a member of an affluent Presbyterian Church in the Northwest suburbs of Chicago say to me that he had just learned how the church was so much more outspoken on social issues back in the sixties and how he understood preachers are unable to do this today. He further knew that many theological seminaries in the sixties were taking a strong stand on social issues such as the Vietnam War and the civil rights movement. Today this has changed to the point that a preacher would not dare preach on such an issue, in that people would not like it and make it difficult for a minister with this theological perspective to stay in the pulpit. It appears that ministry has moved from the outward social change perspective to the inward spiritual psychological perspective. Today people want to feel good and you can't feel good if the preacher is going to confront you with issues that are not comfortable to hear and perhaps even make you feel guilty. It is also important that the church grow in numbers if the preacher is to be "successful" which lends itself to becoming more entertaining.

In the late afternoon of my life I have come to see that change doesn't come very quickly or easily, especially if it has anything to do with the economy, which most everything does. The politicians can preach all they want on raising teachers' salaries, providing more education, helping the homeless, providing better care for the mentally ill, and turning more of our guns into plow shares but it's only rhetoric. When I vote, I vote for rhetoric, nothing more. Most people would say that I have gotten cynical, but it's not so, I have just gotten more realistic. There is a big difference between being cynical and being realistic. Being realistic means you have lived long enough to sort out the bull shit from the truth that sets people free. This doesn't mean that voting is not important. It's very important! Voting for rhetoric means you like what you hear and it's a way of giving a sort of political amen even though it most likely will not come to fruition. Loving and enjoying the people at the commune is kind of like this, knowing that it was too good to be true, but nevertheless giving it a big amen.

Just as the hippies of the 60's have become yuppies so has the social conscious clergy become a "spiritual director" which is safe, playing right into the mentality of the yuppie or the baby boomer. The church is not the same church as it was in the 60's and early 70's where there still seemed to be a concern for those who are poor, questioning war and especially the value of nuclear weaponry, and racial relations. For eleven years I served as an associate pastor of a large church in the Northwest suburbs of Chicago where almost everyone wants: one, to know they have the truth and two, to be happy. There is little room in their lives for anything other than working hard to make much money and to give all they possibly can to their children. In the American suburb it is almost impossible to tell the difference between a child's parent and his or her buddy, between a pastor and one's best friend, and the preacher and one who tells intriguing stories and gives comforting words to support a greedy society. Here in the suburbs those who are different or hold different views are shunned and often shamed. There is no place for the gay or lesbian individual within the church since, according to the suburban interpretation, homosexuality is sinful and therefore unacceptable. A new member of the church shared with me that she quickly perceived that there was no acceptance of the gay or lesbian person in this community and that they would be received coolly, if at all, by this congregation. She only smiled saying, "They will change in due time." This woman has a grown son who is gay. She knew the feeling of this congregation because she held the same views until she experienced a gay son who confronted her with her prejudices, shallowness and conditional love. The gay son became a gift from God which has lifted her to a new level allowing her a freedom she never before felt as a child of God.

The suburban church needs to hear such stories of people who have been transformed by what they once viewed as ugliness and shame and now have been given new life.

Dale and Joyce were delightful people and a light that shown in the suburban church darkness. Dale carried much pain from his military service as an English paratrooper during World War II, yet he carried it well and with great faith, demonstrated by his love for all people, providing hope in an often-discouraging world. I had the privilege of knowing this family in both their pain and in their joy. This family called on me when their retarded daughter, Mandy, died and again when Dale died a few years later. Now they lie together in side-by-side graves while enjoying all the blessings of the Lord. While gathering with Joyce and her three sons they told a wonderfully unforgettable story about Dale.

The family was at the kennel to get a dog for the family. Before they began looking Dale made it clear that they were to pick out the ugliest dog they could find. And they did. Buster is ugly but he is loved. Such love transcends all difference and all ugliness and transforms us into the people that God has called us to be.

This story demonstrates the very heart of the Gospel and yet we often continue to want only the pedigree, the most valuable in worldly terms and the most productive and outwardly beautiful. The church is too much this way, not allowing itself to experience the ugly, the different, and especially the unacceptable.

It's interesting just how much the words, communion, commune, communicate and community are similar in interpretation until we allow prejudice, dogma, politics and culture to get in the way. All four of these words hold in common the idea of being common, close, sharing, to make known and to be known, celebration, intimacy, deep understanding, to impart, to be sympathetic, likeness, public, ownership and fellowship. We are often the ones who determine with whom and where we will demonstrate these attributes, which is to the deployment of those who are most like ourselves. A pastor friend of mine once said to me, "Tom, everyone wants to know they have the truth and to be happy." At what cost?

The commune in that river bottom of Eastern Kentucky meant so much to me because I perceived it as a place where one could be him or her self. Here there was no pretense but rather people who were grounded in love, understanding and appreciation of one another. Just perhaps this is what "being at home" is all about. Margaret Kornfeld says it well.

> In community, we can tell our story. We can become more experienced in saying what we really mean. By being listened to, we can know more fully who we are. The words "communicate", "community", and "communion" have similar meanings. When we communicate, we are in deep relationship, communion, with others. We give. We receive. We do this with our total being – body, mind and soul. We think and we feel. We are whole. We are ourselves. 1

We can perhaps all remember, as children, times when parents or other adults would encourage us to just be ourselves. I would often get this kind of response after expressing disappointment or anger over not being accepted by my peers. When I would express confusion over just how to approach a difficult situation, the answer it seems would always be 'just be yourself'. I would often say to myself – "What does that mean"? It seemed to me that the people who were themselves were often made fun of as being nerds and too often ostracized. Much like the people at the commune.

In the last few years before my retirement I began thinking increasingly how I have been programmed to think a certain way, to hold to ideals and beliefs that are held by most of those around me, friends, associates, comrades in ministry and those who are dependent upon me and how much recognition I need from others. It was like I was in a box and as long as I stayed in that box all was well, or was it? I was so good at this that most people would not even believe, if I told them how dependent I was. A lot of people would make the statement; "Tom really acts outside of the box." Then a friend shared a book with me written by Steven Harrison entitled, *Doing Nothing, Coming to the End of the Spiritual Search.* Harrison demonstrated to me how unnecessarily hard I was working for approval and in the process being something less than human. It was not until after retirement that I came to this recognition realizing what a burden I was carrying. Never trying to offend anyone and staying within the parameters of the faith and beliefs of the church even though I strongly thought differently. Harrison's words speak directly to my heart and soul when he writes: "It is striking how relieved we are when we give up the burden of our acquired spirituality and all its dogma." 2

Yet, I wonder if my need to not offend anyone is really a part of my Appalachian genes that is addressed well by my friend Loyal Jones.

> We will go to great lengths to keep from offending others, even sometimes appearing to agree with them when in fact we do not. It is more important to us to get along and have a good relationship with other persons than it is to make our true feelings known. Mountaineers will give the appearance of agreeing to attend all sorts of meetings that they have no intention of going to, just because they want to be polite. Of course, this personalism is one of the reasons that those who work for confrontation politics often fail in Appalachia. We are extremely reluctant to confront anyone and alienate him, if we can get out of it. If however, the issues are important enough, we will take a stand.3

When I retired the most difficult thing I had to come to grips with was my identity. Whenever I had made a move in the past I always had an instant identity. I was the pastor or the associate pastor or the director of the pastoral counseling center, or sometimes the preacher. I knew who I was and everyone else knew who I was. There was never any question about who I was and what I was to do.

Steven Harrison addressed this whole issue for me in this funny little story.

> After many long sessions, the psychiatrist told his patient," You're cured!" "Big deal" said the patient, "When I came to you I was Napoleon, now I'm nobody." 4

I felt the same as this patient except for me it was retirement that was to be so wonderful. Before retirement I was something – I had an identity, not as Napoleon or even Jesus Christ, but as an associate pastor, a pastoral counselor. Now that I have arrived, been cured and received my reward, am I to be happy? I was an associate pastor and pastoral counselor. Now I am nobody. Thanks a lot! The structure of the self requires identification. Without the sense of being something, the idea of self collapses.

With the collapse of the self there is nothing left but the expression of freedom. Such freedom is not without fear. Who will I be now? What will I do? What identity will I take on? I began attending a church, which my wife and I enjoyed a great deal identifying with the social and theological expression that we heard Sunday after Sunday. I still had no idea what role I would take in this community. I visited the pastor who after much patient listening suggested I take on the role of "creative floundering" knowing that soon or later I would find the right place for me. This was good advice and at last I felt I had come to the end of my spiritual search and could get into doing nothing, which has been an experience of freedom. I no longer have to do anything or be anything. And that feels good.

My experience with the small *commune* in Lee County keeps before me what genuine Christian wholeness is all about. First, a sense of wholeness that involves not only commune where one can be at home among friends, who for the most part believe and think alike, but, secondly, to live in *community*, among neighbors who are very different, finding ourselves not excluded from the world but very much a part of the world: a community where we share the rich gifts that have been given to us through our faith in God. Third, is the all-important need for *communication* that we might hear and be heard, that healing might take place. Fourth, where *communion* is experienced – the breaking of bread together, an interactive reminder and visible sign of God's grace. We have seen how wholeness is most clearly represented in the number or symbol four. Here in these four important aspects of our life is found wholeness, holiness or healing that is most essential for people of faith.

Some might see living in a commune as socialism, with negative connotations, yet it is a way of living molded by the early Christians (Acts 4:32–5:11) and a molding that we might need to take more seriously today. When elderly parents are miles apart from their children and young families need the wisdom of the elderly such a model might need to be more closely examined. When I retired and moved to Berea, Kentucky I would have more than welcomed such a model had it been available. In this model the members of the commune would pool their resources to take care of the needs of each other – health care, sickness, birth, death, and all other aspects of life's joys and sorrows.

Our stories are extremely important. Life might have little meaning without stories, the vehicle that carries the meaning of the soul, that which gives speech to experiences that speak deeper than the intellect with even a larger affect upon those who listen. For the person of faith stories take on special meaning with the community of faith. This is seen most clearly with Jesus who knew the power of a story or parable. Creeds are summations of the adventures of Christ, the God-man. The Psalmist expresses how God is alive and at work with his people, or distant and inactive. There are experiences of deliverance or freedom, punishment or how people have experienced discrimination and expression of anger or awe in response to God's behavior. The letter of First John begins with the author sharing a story that has been told to him, redemptive events for which he is profoundly grateful; a story that changed his life and links him to a community that shares both his memory and the experience of being joyously changed.

All of us are graced. The Word of Life has come to us through our parents, the neighborhood, the church, therapies, and marriages. In stories we find three major players. First is the storyteller who engages the listeners with heartfelt drama bringing to life significant players in the story. Second is God who, lovingly and playfully, invites us into our own growth experience consciously or unconsciously. Third is the listener. All three are woven within the fabric of a story, a divine choreography that is often done so well that the characters blend in a dance that stirs the heart and changes our lives forever. This is not just the skillful work of the Apostle, Psalmist or Jesus, but also the very soul work of all of us. When I was a teenager back in the fifties I was rather rebellious and often ran with a group of friends of the like sort. One evening we ran out of gas with no money to purchase more. One of the boys had the idea that siphoning gas from a parked car would be cool. We thought we had done this with great skill without any of us getting too much gasoline in our mouths or suffocating from gasoline fumes.

> All went well until the police pulled us over and arrested us for burglary. We were placed in jail. By morning all the fathers had come for their sons except for my father who didn't come for me until the next day. When he did come he said, "Let's go home son."

> Out of my distress I called on the Lord, the Lord answered me and set me in a broad place.

> *Psalm* 118:5 (NRSV)

The Hebrew word for distress is *mesar* with rich meaning in that the Hebrew people spoke in whole mouthfuls. *Mesar* not only means distress but can also mean 'tight spot' or 'hemmed in' or 'in a corner'. In my story I was in *mesar*, in a 'tight spot' or we might say 'in jail' – restricted and bound. But "...the Lord set me in a *broad place*." Another whole mouth-full Hebrew word – *broad place* in Hebrew is *yasha*, which connotes safety and security. With *yasha* there is spacious space, lots of room – a figure of speech used for deliverance. When the Hebrew people were 'hemmed in' in Egypt they were promised *broad land*.

My father was a wise man in that he allowed me to both experience *mesar and Yasha;* not rescuing too quickly and yet when he did, allowing me to feel the *broad place* provided by being my father; allowing me space to catch my God given breath after appropriately and necessarily feeling the full effects of being "hemmed in" or literally 'in jail' Then if we read further in Psalm 118 we find out why God sets us in *broad places*. It's because God *delights* in us. It's because the Lord is *for us* – he is *on our side*. We would do well to dwell upon the importance of delighting in our children, both young and old alike, and look for ways of holding in balance both *mesar* and *yasah*. I hear too many stories from children and adults of how they are unnecessarily *hemmed in* or *bound* or shamed by parents who seek to totally define and orchestrate their lives. As parents and grandparents we would do well to listen more to the stories of our children and to anticipate God's holy playfulness. Brian Grant in his book *A Theology for Pastoral Psychotherapy*, subtitled 'God's Play in Sacred Places', says that holy playfulness is,

> Not a playfulness that trivializes, but one that massively enjoys the beauty of the world while not taking itself seriously at all, simultaneously being a superb steward of itself as contributor to that world. Such a God interacting playfully with such a world is all at once admiring, enjoying, luring, teasing and simulating growth in all that God loves.5

In my story it's difficult to separate out the characters and their attributes. Once I came to realize that this story took place on God's landscape and that God's playfulness was all around me with large measures of grace, the characters blended and complimented one another so well that I could not well define them. Within this story my Dad, the community, the church and God seemed as one, dancing about with healing dimensions that set me free. I often wondered if Dad felt any of the same feelings as I. I strongly suspect he did. The more I tell and retell this story the more convinced I become. Brian Grant has these words that are so appropriate to our stories, saying,

> The privilege is visible in two aspects: the joy of seeing the other assuming full stature as a child of God, while knowing one's own exaltations by means of participating in that healing; and the invitation into segments of reality from which one is otherwise excluded by social position, education, status, race, citizenship, gender, or age. 6

In my story it's difficult to determine the blessed from the blesser, the befriended from the friend, the saved from the savior and the healed from the healer. When we experience God's play in sacred spaces we become the bearer of being one to the other, "Little Christ" in Martin Luther's sense, and are thus incredibly privileged. Let us be about looking for God's play in sacred spaces.

In many communities are carillons, a wonderful electronic piece of technology, which can play bells or musical pieces that can be broadcast all over the neighborhood, college campus, seminary, garden areas or a number of communities that appreciate music. It often gives a lovely effect for weddings and such but the drawback is the lack of human effort or engagement involved except for the talented musician that operates the various controls that make such beautiful music. Too often there is no one playing at all but rather a fine tuned computerized instrument set to turn the carillon on and off at particular times of the day. In small European towns the beautiful ringing of bells is still performed manually at noon followed by the closing of stores that the people might take leisure. The ringing of bells is often calling for the community to 'sit a spell', taking rest within a busy day. I envision a young boy or girl being pulled up and down by the weight and swing of the bell while a proud father, grandfather or other adult watches. Then story telling might follow in such sacred spaces where God dances and delights in us as we delight in one another experiencing *yasha*. Such scenarios of God's playfulness are not possible in our society of hard work and commercialism and so we have to consciously search the divine landscape for God's playfulness. This can be done only as we listen carefully to our children's *mesar*, their stories of distress while together we experience *yasha* – the broad space of safety and security, that space where we experience blessedness, that space in which we are delighted and allowed to grow and experience healing and wholeness, that space where God lures and teases us into adventure and new possibilities as we take pleasure in God and one another within the context of our families and communities.

I have friends that are on a journey across the United States on a bicycle built for five. Bill and Amarins have three little girls all under the age of seven. They left from Rockcastle County, Kentucky and their trip is to take them to Florida, across the southern United States and then up the West Coast into Alaska. They plan to travel a total of 7000 miles over a period of about two years. This is like a traveling commune, living off the land and by the graciousness of many friends and communities along the way. They will have a lot of experiences of both *mesar* and *yasha*. They have already experienced the sacred, the playfulness of God in broad spaces but also the distress of storms and flat tires, and they have a long way to go before arriving at their destination.

For many playfulness in broad places is found to be difficult. Control and power is so strong that it can narrowly define our space and restrict our playfulness. If we need to always have a plan, and to know what the results or outcome will be, our lives will be so predictable that nothing new will come about. We will only become caught in the nets of the status quo. Such lives will surely leave us restricted and bound up in the familiar, the known and that which we feel to be safe.

When I retired I complained that I no longer knew who I was or what my role in life was to be now that I was no longer in a clearly defined role of ministry. And then, I read Eckhart Tolle who stated, "If you can be absolutely comfortable with not knowing who you are, then what's left is who you are, the being behind the human, a field of pure potentiality rather than something that is already defined."[7] I began to think about how this might be applied to communities or faith groups. Just perhaps we have such clearly defined rules, regulations, and doctrinal statements that we no longer know who we are or what we believe beyond such roles or identity. Would we dare become so comfortable with not knowing who we are and become a field of pure potentiality?

The following quote from Eckhart Tolle might well be used as a tool for evaluating not only ourselves but the community in which we live and play.

> Give up defining yourself – to yourself or to others. You won't die. You will come to life. And don't be concerned with how others define you. When they define you, they are limiting themselves, so it's their problem. Whenever you interact with people, don't be there primarily as a function or a role, but as a field of conscious Presence.
>
> Why does the ego play roles? Because of one unexamined assumption, one fundamental error, one unconscious thought. That thought is: I am not enough. Other unconscious thoughts follow: I need to play a role in order to get what I need to be fully myself: I need to get more so that I can be more. But you cannot be more than you are because underneath your physical and psychological form, you are and will always be inferior to some, superior to others. In essence, you are neither inferior nor superior to anyone. True self-esteem and true humility arise out of

that realization. In the eyes of the ego, self-esteem and humility are contradictory. In truth, they are one and the same. 8

As I look back on my experience with the people at the commune I wonder if Tolle's *giving up on role-playing* was not a psychology they were acting out in community. Tolle's idea of being a *field of conscious presence* seems to define these young people. Just perhaps that is why my family and I enjoyed them so much.

I wondered too if this was not what my father enjoyed about people and himself, this idea of living in a *field of conscious presence.* Dad just enjoyed people as they were in the present moment with no pretense or role-playing. What a wonderful model for the family or the church to follow.

TO FIND ONE'S GROUND

To find one's ground
is to cultivate the soul
that one's richness is known
embraced, appreciated and safe.
The experience of grace
in commune found.

To find one's ground,
reaching out to neighbors all around,
to give abundantly,
to share the grace received,
moving beyond the self,
in community found.

To find one's ground,
listening and revealing the self,
especially to words not spoken.
Differences appreciated – uniqueness encouraged,
to know more fully who we are –
in divine/human dialog we are found.

To find one's ground,
surprises of grace,
unexpected healing,
being at home,
eating heartily – drinking deeply –
communion found.

COME SIT A SPELL

Weary from life's strivings
Expectations abound
Trust an empty sound
Traditions sliding away
Listening a lost talent
Come sit a spell

Looking in all the wrong places
Racing on freeways
Crowded trains
McDonald's, soccer and cell phones
Yet left alone
A voice not so distant inviting
Come sit a spell

How much is enough
A question engaging
Might leave the soul searching
And hearts pounding
For something more
A voice from deep within inviting
Come sit a spell

Living is what we are doing with or without our philosophies, our meditation techniques, our religions. Living is the expression of relatedness of all life. We need not fear it. We can simply live. We can relax.

Steven Harrison

GO SLOW

In the southern part of the United States life is generally slower which can be delightful most of the time, but frustrating at other times, even to the natives. In the Deep South this might be the result of the extremely hot and muggy weather, and out of necessity to conserve energy folk have learned to stay in the shade. Sometimes this life style can be confused with laziness, taking on the nature of the three-toed sloth in the Amazon Rain Forest that moves so slowly it is necessary to focus on them for a time even to see if they are alive. In reality, these creatures are intoxicated from the leaves they constantly eat leaving them in a stupor or drunken state. This is not uniquely the situation in Eastern Kentucky since slothfulness can be experienced in people anywhere in the world. Yet there is a real sense of 'laid backness' in these hills that is noticeable. Perhaps it's more than just 'laid-backness', but rather a posture that has been acquired over the years, an attitude that must be taken seriously if a relationship is to be established with the mountain people.

Saint Helens is a sleepy little town in Lee County that is quickly passed through on the way to Jackson. Saint Helens could, and probably would, be overlooked unless you have reason to expect it. On the highway you would find a few modest houses clustered together with a road veering off to the left. In this part of the country it is rare to give directions as north or south, east or west, but rather off the road to the left, or up a hollow, off the Old Jackson Road or up on Spencer Ridge. Many times, perhaps most of the time, directions are given according to the lay of the land and/or the location of someone's farm or family home. If you didn't know the people who live, or have lived, in these hills you most likely would not make any sense out of directions you got from the local people. If Saint Helens is to be found you must go slow or you will surely pass it by, especially since the real heart of the town is up this road to the left that takes one to a beautiful hilltop with old homes and a run down business district. This is where the post office, hardware store, and Christian Church are located and a few old homes, most of which have not seen paint in years. You might take one look at this community and draw the conclusion that it was a dead town left to the weather and critters. At first glance you would think that everyone had just up and left everything as it stands. One might wonder if time had stopped in this small town, left to the past, with infrequent memories and without thoughts of it ever being brought back to life. The only real sign of life was back down the hill to the main road. It was at this intersection that the Presbyterian Church, the general store and gas station were located.

George Combs was an elderly mountain man who lived with his wife, Nola, in the oldest house in Saint Helens dating back to before the Civil War. When I first visited the Combs house I wondered if anyone really lived here in that it appeared abandoned. The yard was unkempt and there was no sign that the house had ever been painted. I felt as if I was visiting an abandoned community that existed perhaps a hundred years ago. There was no way I expected to experience any kind of life in this house (or even in the whole community) that was built off the highway up on this beautiful hill overlooking some of the best farm land in the county. I walked up on the old porch and made my way to the door on which I knocked gently out of fear I would wake the dead or tear down the door. Nola came to the door with a big smile and quickly welcomed me into their home. With great joy and enthusiasm Nola introduced me to her husband, an elderly man who was tall, very thin, unshaven with clothes appearing to be about two sizes too large. All around George were newspapers, books and magazines. I saw The Wall Street Journal, U.S. News and World Report, Time Magazine and numerous other reading materials that appeared so out of place. I felt as if I was back to the future. I soon learned that going slow in this home did not mean to be backward or misinformed. I quickly learned that George was a delightful, well-educated, currently informed agnostic that had never attended church nor did he ever plan to attend. I also learned that Nola had great expectations of every new preacher, that in some way they could get George to see the light and come around to accepting the Lord and attend church. This was just not going to happen! Nola loved George and was most proud of his intellectual pursuits; therefore she never gave up trying.

I never tired of visiting George whom I found to be a breath of fresh air in an intellectually stifled community. It was always amazing just how much he knew not only about history, but also about current events. Just perhaps he was as starved for this type of intellectual stimulation as I was. I would guess George was in his mid seventies when I knew him so well but yet he acted as a young man who couldn't learn enough and always wanted to know my opinions and views. George was truly a man of wisdom, not of having much knowledge but possessing sagacity, leaving me refreshed and respected. The relationship I had with George was one you wish all young men could experience and I have often wondered if this is not why Nola really wanted me to visit with her husband. The very man who did not attend church appeared to me to be quite godly, non judgmental and extremely pastoral in so many ways.

George had a presence about him that is rarely seen in

the church, which could well be why he had no desire to attend. After all Jesus didn't appear to have any real desire to attend church and, had his most effective ministry sitting around wells with women and aboard boats with fishers. After visiting George I often felt as if I had had a holy experience with a man who put listening before talking and always made me feel that I was of importance. Young men today desperately need a George in their lives, which might be a reason to restore the front porch or the pot bellied stove in the general store. This just might be what the church ought to be providing in this postmodern world and yet the amount of imagination, creativity and time acquired seems out of the question. Yet the institutional church cannot contain such an icon as George, or the street preacher, but such holy moments must be experienced in more unique ways as Moses did through the burning bush. George was just where he needed to be and Nola's obsession with his lack of religion was just that – her obsession. We are so quick to get people like George to attend the church and yet when you meet a person like George you can't help but wonder if God doesn't already have a special place in his heart for them and that his attending church is for our own satisfaction.

Meanwhile at the bottom of the hill at the intersection of the Jackson highway was the general store and gas station. This had become the hub of the community, if there was such a thing, in Saint Helens. I soon learned this was the real source of information if you could have the patience to wait for it. A real part of Appalachia's slowness, laid back or even aloofness has much to do with its sense of woundedness by big coal, gas and oil companies from the Northeast. Around the turn of the century these companies came into Appalachia knowing of the rich fields of coal and oil that existed under the land. Many of these companies took advantage of the people's lack of education and knowledge of the richness of their land, and had them sign contracts, called 'broad-form deeds', for very little money giving unlimited rights to coal and oil. The people also worked for the coal companies who paid them in tokens that could be spent only at the company store. We might be reminded of Tennessee Ernie Ford's popular song, 'I Sold my Soul to the Company Store.' One has only to drive through Appalachia to see the scars, not only on the mountains from strip mining but also to experience the scars on the people's hearts, minds and souls. Such injury has caused the mountain people to be leery, to go slow and not greet people too openly and quickly before knowing their intentions. Just perhaps this is a way to get a little bit back in control of their lives which many feel had been taken from them.

When I was visiting the Soviet Union back in 1988 I found many of the people rarely smiled and were unfriendly with blank faces. I made friends with a young woman in Kiev who later said to me, 'You might think that the people are lazy and unfriendly but they are not lazy or unfriendly, they just don't care'. In the face of oppression and depression it is easy to get to the place where you just don't care. In many ways this is what has happened to the people of Appalachia. Of course this is not true of all the people and yet many fall within this category. As a pastoral counselor I have seen a number of individuals referred through a free medical clinic who are depressed out of no fault of their own but rather have become victimized by loss of job, loss of family members and physically and emotionally abused by 'lovers', spouses, employees and family members. Too often the church adds to their depression by suggesting that they do not have enough faith in God. Such preaching only makes the depressed people feel more depressed and of little value as they withdraw into isolation. Like the people of the old Soviet Union it is difficult to trust others and take a warm attitude towards the stranger when you have been taken advantage of through the years by so many who have pretended to have good intentions. It's enough to make a person go slow and not expect too much too soon but rather remain highly skeptical.

While serving a small church in Lee County I would

occasionally receive calls from church groups in cities around the country who wanted to arrange to visit Appalachia. Too often these were groups who found it a novelty to visit one of the poorest regions of the country. Such groups wanted to come and work on our churches or community buildings feeling it was the Christian thing to do, as if we were a mission field. We were often referred to as the 'home mission field.' This would make us feel even more depressed. I would suggest to these groups that they invite us to their church and community that we might be of service to them. This suggestion was never taken seriously and I never received an invitation because it just never fit their idea of the Appalachian people nor the manner in which they understood themselves within the context of doing or receiving missionary assistance.

These groups would need to be guests in the homes of the church members. The exposure of these people to one another was of great spiritual and therapeutic value but convincing them of this was no easy matter. Appalachian people may be poor but they are not stupid for they realized exactly what I was asking them to do – to have a person of means from a totally different culture live in their home, a home with no running water and an outside toilet. Upon making this request anxieties would only rise. Molly who was in her early sixties and a widow of about five years lived in a lovely mountain home on the side of a mountain in Lee County. To get to her house it was necessary to park just off the road in a small space carefully cut out for parking. It was best to visit in dry weather in that this small parking area was just off the paved road beside a steep embankment and extremely muddy after a rain. It wouldn't take much to just slide right off over the embankment. It could be most treacherous to anyone not familiar with this part of the country. To get to Molly's house one had to take a narrow path cut out along the side of the mountain. From the front porch was a beautiful view overlooking the two-lane highway and mountains that rose just beyond. Molly's home was simple with none of the modern conveniences that most homes had then. A well provided water for the hand pump that was located in the kitchen by the sink and nearby was a washstand with a bowl of water and towel neatly hanging alongside of the stand. The house was furnished with what most of us today would only see in antique shops and would most likely pay a high price to have in our own homes. Molly seemed to always have a pot of pinto beans cooking on the potbelly stove, which was often customary in Appalachian homes.

When I approached Molly about keeping a young woman who was visiting with a group from Seattle she was most reluctant arguing that her home was not nice enough and not adequately furnished for such a guest. It was only after much persuasion that Molly finally gave in but only if I brought the woman at a particular time. We set the day and time when I would introduce this young woman to Molly. The group from Seattle arrived a day early and I made the big mistake of taking Molly's guest to her on the day before the date and time we had agreed upon. When Molly came to the door she was most upset and obviously angry with me for breaking our agreement. Thanks to the young woman who began making over Molly's home saying how privileged it was going to be to stay in such a beautiful place. The woman even made over the washstand and other pieces of furniture that she could see from the front room. This was more than I ever expected and I remained grateful to the young woman for the manner in which she handled my introduction to Molly, which immediately diffused all of Molly's anger and anxiety concerning this houseguest.

I am reminded of, Joe Ikunyua, a fellow student at Louisville Presbyterian Seminary who was visiting from Kenya, Africa. This was during the civil rights' movement and race riots all across the country. While African Americans were demonstrating and holding rallies in Louisville I asked Joe if he felt any connection with the African Americans and if he had joined them in any of their demonstrations. I will never forget his answer. "The only thing I have in common with the African American is color. I do not fully understand their passion and therefore must earn the right to speak.

Make not speech cheap

Among expensive voices

Speaking of heartfelt convictions

Shouting for justice from deep places

Soul mates know their voices

Earn the right to speak

Listen to the voices

Emerging from the collective soul

Earn the trust before making a fuss

Make not speech cheap

Yet another example comes to mind of how we fail to realize who we are, where we are and the rights we have or don't have. Bill was an Alcohol Counselor under my supervision while I was Clinical Director of the Chatham Clinic for Alcoholism in Savannah, Georgia. Bill was excited about a trip he had made to West Virginia and fully enjoyed the mountains, the towns, and the rivers of this wonderful state. Yet he was puzzled that the people did not talk to him more. He said it was like he was suspect and they were reluctant to volunteer any information about themselves. He said the people came across as cold and indifferent. There is something very spiritual about all this, isn't there? Something that has to do with injury, trust and respect, something about taking others and ourselves more seriously rather than making assumptions. Something about earning the right to speak, imposing ourselves upon another's space or to even earn the right to engage with another until we know who this person is and where we are in the sacred landscape of God' people.

Sacred space

A gift of God

Opened and quickly closed

Disrespected

Now wait your turn

Earn the right to enter

Walk softly

Listen carefully

Know where you are

I loved to visit the general store and gas station when I was the preacher of the small Presbyterian Church just across the road. The store and the people were most enjoyable in the winter months when the "potbelly" stove was stoked well with coal giving off delightful welcoming warmth. When you enter such a store in this part of the country it's advisable to remain silent – I mean don't even say 'hello, 'howdy' or even grunt. I would let the people take the initiative as I helped myself to a moon pie and orange soda in preparation to join others seated around the stove on empty wooden soda crates. Sometimes there was just silence and other times I would join in the listening of some stories that had been told over and over and every time they were told they became more exaggerated. Then someone would say in a nonchalant fashion, "How'ya doin', preacher?" Most often a good response would be: 'fair to midlin', or 'all right, I reckon.'

In Appalachia folk were never good or bad but rather somewhere in between. It's not unusual to hear the response "tolerable well" when anyone asked how you were doing. Life is not great nor is it terrible, but rather life is that which is tolerated, and for the most part ain't bad, all things considered. This kind of language is most telling about the people in these mountains. It's an honest response to a greeting and if more of us were more authentic with our responses we might choose "fair to midlin" over the use of 'fine'. 'Fine' most often comes with a mask that seeks to hide our real feelings about how we feel about life at that given moment. Most people outside of Appalachia don't have the right or privilege to go about tolerating life or to be just 'fair to midlin.' If we were to make a statement like this in Chicago people might just move away from you as if you had the plague. The message we constantly get in Appalachia is 'go slow' – you don't have to be fine all the time. It is all right, and even preferred, not to have it all together. Life is not something that can be mastered, but rather lived in tension with the full realization that we experience both ecstasy and discipline, both good and evil, and to be 'fair to midlin' is in a real way claiming our middle ground, knowing we have arrived and yet still on a journey. Is this not the same tension that Christians lived under two thousand years after the Resurrection? That the kingdom has come and yet the kingdom is coming? There are those things we can enjoy but there is also more to come for which we can only wait.

When I was out making pastoral calls or just dropping by for a quick visit it was not at all unusual to hear the statement of 'come sit a spell.' When people said this it was inviting. You knew they meant what they said apart from just trying to be polite. It was like they were saying, 'What's your hurry?' or 'Let's chat a while'. Life is short – go slow – sit down – let's be together for a few minutes in a relaxed, informal and enjoyable manner.

"Come sit a spell" is a statement among the mountain people that can never or should never be forgotten. It's an invitation to go slow. It's an invitation that has deep spiritual meaning which can only speak to your soul and lower your blood pressure. It's a statement and invitation that we need to hear when road rage is so prominent, and when we are filling our days with forty-eight hours, and each member of the family is going a separate way, seldom experiencing a common meal. "Come sit a spell" is a spoken oasis in our dry and weary journey through the desert of life where we only reach out for mirages that leave us empty and angry. 'Come sit a spell' without one plea – pull up a pop crate, a rocking chair or come sit on the porch swing. Go Slow.

Envision the church as a building with one continuous wide porch running around on all four equal sides filled with swings and rocking chairs. Envision a large yard with deep, plush, green grass growing all around and a sign in the yard reading, 'Come sit a spell.' Envision people sitting and conversing, laughing and crying with the voices of children playing. Envision our sport-utility vehicles parked with cool manifolds in the middle of a workday. Come and take refuge. 'Spell' means a period of rest or relief from activity. Is this not Sabbath? Come take Sabbath and know that this is a holy place, the very place in which you sit a spell. Wait and know that you are not God.

Richard A. Swenson, M.D. Associate Professor at the University of Wisconsin Medical School has written a book entitled Margin, which encourages us to build more margins into our lives that we might more seriously evaluate time and space in our overloaded lives.2 Dr. Swenson suggests we stand in the longest line at the bank or grocery store and to park our cars in the farthest part of the parking lot and walk to the Mall or Wal-Mart. Swenson has only one tie and one suit which simplifies his life and lowers his stress level. This way he does not have to go through the stressful process each day of deciding what to wear. This might seem a little extreme in our fast paced world and yet what better way to work toward the "come sit a spell" approach to our busy lives. Just perhaps we might go slow enough to allow us to more fully entertain the concept of 'come sit a spell'.

When I would schedule a meeting of the Elders they would not attend. During the week I would see them and ask why they were not at the meeting and they would respond with, "Oh, Preacher, you should have given me a call, I was just home watching T.V." In Beattyville I often found little use for a watch or even a calendar. Time and space was of little concern. I found that the best place for our meetings was at the local drug store, which was owned by members of the Christian Church. Each morning a good representation of Presbyterians as well as others would gather for coffee. It was here that decisions could be made as well as announced to the community. This appeared to be the best way to conduct church business since everyone in the community knew everyone else's business anyway. No newspaper was necessary – the word would beat me back to the church.

The message was always the same, 'Go slow preacher and if you need anything just let us know'. Years later while ministering in a large church in the Chicago area I found myself often recalling these words, "go slow" and "come sit a spell". While ministering to young parents I would often suggest they build margins into their lives rather than fill the days with business from morning to night. I would suggest they allow one hour longer in taking their son or daughter to soccer practice and then drop by one of the parks and talk with their children or to have some unstructured time for them to run and play with other children. I was suggesting that they go slow. This idea never caught on in that these young parents were too caught up in "productivity" and felt that such free time was wasteful and had no real value.

My wife and I were fortunate to live in a Chicago Suburban neighborhood where everyone made it a point to get acquainted and would frequently celebrate holidays together. Once a year we would have a block party, which was like a big potluck dinner outside on the street. I was often told that this was highly unusual and that most people in large city suburbs did not even know their next-door neighbor.

Folk in the neighborhood would often sit on their porch when the weather was pleasant. Conversations took place back and forth across the street, on the sidewalks and in the yards and on porches. Most houses in the neighborhood had porches, which I found most inviting. Our house did not have a front porch but rather a brick entrance with steps where we would often sit in the evenings. It was not long until neighbors came over to join us in conversation. I found the children to be comfortable with all the neighbors and would play in everybody's yard. I felt we all looked after the children's interests, as it should be. This neighborhood was inviting by its very nature, communicating by action the message of "go slow" and "come sit a spell" – a little Appalachia in a well-to-do Chicago suburb, Unique and enjoyable.

A word of caution might be necessary at this point so that going slow is not confused with being lazy or non-productive. It is not unusual for busy and highly productive people to view 'sitting a spell' or 'going slow' with being non productive. Perhaps this is an issue of values. Often we find the idea that what is important or valued is something material. If our activities are not producing more money in order that we can have more things, then such activities are of no worth. This way of thinking does not take into account the cultural and health value of 'going slow'. Nor does it always consider the social aspects and pure enjoyment of going slow. We often hear the statement that we ought to stop and smell the roses. Well, going slow or just purely sitting a spell could be a likely comparison.

ACCEPTANCE

Earth is warmed gentle and quietly,
as sun slowly breaks through the fog.
From the night, rest is broken,
not with a shout but as a whisper,
moving the soul into a new day.

Hold the moment,
that it might speak in silence,
as lovers gazing into the eyes of each other,
who need not speak,
knowing it would make for thunder.

Sit quietly and move slowly,
as friends around a warm stove.
Expecting nothing, anticipating everything,
reaping from the experience
of the creative forces moving among us.

Earth is cooling with smooth color
as sun quietly spreads across horizon.
To end the day another way,
only that we might have our say,
is to miss the message of this day.

EAT HALF AS MUCH,
CHEW TWICE AS LONG

DVD's, TV's and video games,
entertainment in a dull world
give me more before I'm bored,
while spirits in crowded airports soar
bringing on rage in an affluent society
that's got to have more.

Eat half as much, chew twice as long,
sounds strange in a world of more,
hunger abounds where plates are filled
souls are searching in all the wrong places
racing without starting, finishing, never
leaving one void within the crowd.

Pretty ladies with stained glass roses,
empty pews with solemn faces,
a limited diet that chews without eating
yet bands play with words displaying.
Senses are filled in pretty ladies –
a lot of eating with limited chewing

Eat half as much, chew twice as long,
bloatedness kills the spirit
while discipline renews and nurtures the soul.
Enjoy the limited,
step aside, let rage go by –
eat half as much, chew twice as long.

My salvation is to hear and respond, for this, my life must be silent. Hence, my silence is my salvation.

Thomas Merton

EAT HALF AS MUCH, CHEW TWICE AS LONG

While trying to provide a ministry as an Associate Pastor in a large church in suburban Chicago I found one of the largest obstacles to good mental and spiritual health to be the rush to have more. A bumper sticker I once read seemed to say it so well, 'He who dies with the most toys wins'. That bumper sticker didn't stay around long, for what was intended as humor became too much of the truth and a dominant life style for most Americans. Hurried lives create high anxiety and anger, keeping us in ill health and robbing us of the ability to relate more effectively and lovingly. If this is called winning I don't think I have any desire to ever entertain what losing might look like. With this kind of winning who needs losing?

This rush to having more is especially prevalent with our defense department as we continue to stock pile more and more nuclear weapons. At the Savannah River Plant just north of Savannah, Georgia, the production of Plutonium, which is highly toxic, has continued to be manufactured at great sacrifice to the environment and to the physical health and reproduction process of both humans and animals. I have heard testimonies of farmers who tell of calves being born with two heads and the unusually high level of cancer being detected in the workers at the Savannah River Plant. While attending a protest rally at the plant site large numbers of local people were angered out of fear they might lose their jobs, therefore establishing counter rallies to support the production of Plutonium. On the drive home I will never forget the response of my friend who stated, "I guess people are too busy making a living than to live." Be it defense or greed it appears we just don't know how much is enough and are unable or unwilling to set limits for our own good.

I remember once just prior to Christmas, when people were frantically shopping in a popular merchandise mart, watching with great interest while waiting for my wife to purchase a few items, the manager came up to me asking if he could be of assistance. I politely stated that I was only waiting for my wife while she shopped and at the same time asked if he was having enough business. He quickly responded, "Oh no, we could always use more business." In return I responded, "How much is enough?" He then walked away from me with a puzzling look on his face.

My father would often tell the family, usually at the dinner table, a story about his brother, Roy, who was a giant of a man and rather than eat to live, Roy lived to eat. Dad would suggest to Roy that he eat half as much and chew it twice as long. As you might guess this did not set well with Roy and he would just eat that much more. I always thought this story applied more broadly than to just the eating of food but rather to much of life itself. We live in an affluent society where it is difficult to set limits, running at a fast pace, overindulging not only in food but also in an abundance of material goods.

While visiting in Austria I found the life style to be much less hurried than it is here in the United States. In many of the cities the church bells would ring at noon at which time the stores would close and the streets became almost void of people. It appeared to be a time not just for lunch but a time to rest and enjoy friends and family. I understand this is the norm for many places in the world. Can you imagine this taking place in the United States? This whole idea of the siesta is about values deeply rooted in tradition. For those parts of the world, which participate in a siesta, there is much value in rest, relaxation and the gathering of friends and family for conversation. Most likely this is a tradition that goes way back into their history and to stray from such tradition would become extremely stressful. Here in the United States values are totally different. We value productivity in which money is the greatest indicator of our hard work. To stop work for rest and enjoyment of friends and family on a daily basis is unimaginable.

I have found only poetry can really express what I experience and deeply feel for a community that knows how to live; community that knows what it is to both work and rest – to enjoy life more fully with friends and neighbors in the midst of a highly commercial society. I experienced this most fully on the Mediterranean coast of Spain within the small community that lived, played and worked around Plaza de Saint Antonio in Vinaros, Spain.

PLAZA DE SANT ANTONIO

A green oasis in community

Lies quiet in early hours

Awaiting the playing laughter of children

Children losing patience with mothers

Not yet ready for the day on the plaza

The morning brings noises of scooters

Families crossing in route to beach

A cool fountain calls forth a new day

While café umbrellas blossom on side walks

Coffee invites waking souls to stay

High burning sun at noonday
Brings the sounds of bells that ring
Closing shop doors
All rest, even the birds on wings
Fountain stops

This green oasis lies quiet now
The sound of a community at rest
With little shade to be found
Preparing for the evening
That will need the energy saved

Within the medium a message found
Behind closed doors and quiet plaza
The best is chosen
Rest and leisure experienced
That life might bloom more fully

With fountain gushing high
A second awakening begins
With bells ringing shop doors open
Children playing around chatting mothers
While grandparents beam on green benches

Josef Pieper states that leisure was established as an essential element in the creation of culture. For Pieper, leisure serves as an attitude of the soul and for inward calm, giving a genuine apprehension concerning the world's reality. Pieper refers to Psalm 46:10 as it is translated from the Septuagint: "Have leisure and know that I am God." The New Revised Standard Version of Psalm 46:10 reads, "Be still, and know that I am God." Yet leisure is even more than stillness, it's more than being unproductive, as our Puritan tradition would have us believe, and more in the vein of experiencing a spiritual capacity for freedom. Leisure is an opportunity to do nothing and yet everything, to engage with God while being disengaging, and perhaps to eat nothing and chew it twice as long.

My daughter graduated from a well known all women's liberal arts college in Charlotte, North Carolina, which attracted a number of young women from wealthy families across the South. Martha found it difficult living with these women in that they put so much emphasis on material things such as fine automobiles, clothing and jewelry. I remember her telling her mother and me of the credit cards her friends had with unlimited spending and how they would go shopping and buy such expensive items. Martha was further appalled by how casually these friends would treat their expensive clothes and jewelry by throwing them in a chair or even in the floor. This was an educational experience alone for Martha in that she not only had to learn how to live with these new friends but also how to integrate this new experience into her own value system that was so different, and do it without becoming angry and resentful. Martha's struggle with this experience became of equal value to her academics and I remain proud of the positive ways in which she responded but most importantly the manner in which she was able to learn from the experience. Martha continued to eat half as much and chew twice as long.

Each year this college would have a father and daughter weekend during which fathers were given a tour of the college and attended various events with their daughters. Of course it was also an opportunity for the college to establish a relationship with fathers who would be able to give generously in the coming years. Being in ministry I was not much of a candidate but nevertheless I always looked forward to this time with Martha. Martha would tell me how anxious many of the girls became about one month before their fathers would arrive. They would express how uncomfortable they were with their fathers and did not know what to do with them. Martha suggested they talk with their fathers, which drew the response, "I don't talk with my father!" As it worked out many of them would go shopping with their father and some would return with expensive clothing and even sports cars. What a contrast to Martha and me enjoying a milk shake at the Dairy Queen.

Joy and I thought it would be handy to have a wall telephone in the kitchen, which would provide needs we felt to be important at this time in our lives – the need to have messages recorded and a receiver that would be mobile allowing us to answer calls from the yard, the car, etc. After installing the phone to a wall jack and to an electrical outlet I soon found it to be a much more difficult process. I got out the manual that came with the phone and soon found that this was a foreign language to me. What was most overwhelming was just how much this small instrument provided. This phone was set up to do almost everything except prepare an evening meal. We both agreed that we didn't need or want all these extras and that we would try to understand how we might go about setting up the parts we did want. Surely together we could get this accomplished. Why should we kid ourselves? We haven't even learned how to operate our VCR even after our engineer son-in-law has explained it to us numerous times. We decided it best to wait until one of our technical minded friends could help us or to seek out a fourteen-year-old. When our friend was able to get the phone up and running, as we wanted he responded, "The phone manufacturers need to know that more is not better." Amen!

Perhaps we have programmed machines to function like we do as persons – not knowing how much is enough, overloading the system to the point we become tired and useless. Josef Pieper puts it in perspective when he writes the following in one of his wonderful books,

...the world of "work" and of the "worker" in a poor, impoverished world, be it ever rich in material goods; for on an exclusively utilitarian basis, on the basis, that is, of the world of "work," genuine wealth, wealth which implies overflowing into superfluities, into unnecessaries, is just not possible.1

Strange words in a world in which we put so much emphasis on work. We are now working more hours than ever before and accumulating more things than any country in the history of the world. It appears we have more gadgets with sophisticated technology that allows us to save more time and do things more efficiently to have more time to work. Physicians are now saying that people are working such long hours that sleep deprivation is taking its toll on their physical and mental health. Therefore we are finding more automobile accidents and people less able to handle anger in a responsible and productive manner. According to Josef Pieper leisure has a strong spiritual dimension and closely associated to the Holy, providing health and wholeness to all of God's creation.

On the other hand, divine worship, of its very nature, creates a sphere of real wealth and superfluity, even in the midst of the direst material want because sacrifice is the living heart of worship. And what does sacrifice mean? It means an offering freely given. It definitely does not involve utility; it is in fact absolutely antithetic to utility. Thus, the act of worship creates a store of real wealth, which cannot be consumed by the workaday world. It sets up an area where calculation is thrown to the winds and goods are deliberately squandered, where usefulness is forgotten and generosity reigns. Such wastefulness is, we repeat, true wealth; the wealth of the feast time. And only in this feast time can leisure unfold and come to fruition.2

Just perhaps true wealth is sitting a spell, wasting time, 'feast time', Sabbath where usefulness is forgotten and generosity prevails. Just perhaps sitting a spell is the opposite of laziness. Just perhaps eating half as much and chewing twice as long is a holy activity and embraces the words of the psalmist when he says, "Have leisure and know that I am God."

I once heard The Reverend Dr. Rene Castellanos of the Ecumenical Seminary in Matanzas, Cuba tell how the United States' boycott has severely handicapped their country and yet they thrive in ways that would have been impossible without the boycott. The Cuban people have had to manage on half as much, or less, in the area of medicine and food. As a result they have become more self-reliant and less prejudiced toward one another. They have very good medical care that is available to everyone. The universities are now open to both the blacks and women where they were not before the revolution. The churches are filled every Sunday, which is quite a contrast to our country and especially in the European countries. The more we have the less reliant we are on God, and the less we contribute to God, and the more we contribute to our own knowledge and ingenuity. The more we have the more defenses we need to keep others from getting it and the less sensitive we are to the poor. Wealth seems to get in the way of really living and to freedom itself in that our stuff begins to own us rather than we owning it. Our stuff begins to control us in that it takes much time and energy to maintain it, store it or protect it in various forms and manners. We also have to work harder and longer to have the money to buy it and maintain it and, in a way, we become slaves to our possessions. No wonder we need God less and less in an affluent society when we have so many other gods that appear to satisfy our needs and demand so much of our attention.

When I was serving on the jury in Chicago with eleven other people I was amazed at how helpless the jurors were without their electronic devices – lap top computers, palm organizers and cell phones. It soon became apparent that I was the only one without such electronic equipment when we were granted various breaks during the day. Jurors were no more out of the jury room than all kinds of electronic sounds were made from the many devices as they began walking the halls or finding a corner in which they could set up office. As for me I only wanted to relax by getting away from such noise and confusion and found myself attracted to some large windows where the sunlight was streaming in upon a wooden bench. It was here that I could relax for a moment before the next round of courtroom activity.

Bob Greene, editorialist for the Chicago Tribune wrote an article entitled "Do you really want to be an office?" Bob tells of a woman in the seat next to him on a plane who was complaining about her husband who was constantly working leaving no time for her or their children. Greene writes,

> The technology had made it possible. With the family's multiple cellular telephones, with his hand-held electronic business organizer, with his home computer linked to his office and to the outside world, it seemed to her that with his success had come something that felt like the opposite of success.

Chicago Tribune, June 26, 2001

This editorial scenario sounds very familiar to any pastor who ministers in the Chicago suburbs. Many workers today are expected to be working twenty-four hours a day. Men and women such as this woman's husband have no free time, no family time and no time in which he is ever off duty. Bob Greene tells of a leading computer manufacturer and software company that sells an advertising promotion piece for just this type of business person. The slogan – which appears over a photo of a human being – is: "I am my office." If we are to have a more enjoyable life and peaceable world to live in we must get out of the way. This is an idea that is for the most part completely foreign to most of us. The mystics understood this for being empty or in poverty of soul providing the room necessary for the very work of God. I think Meister Eckhart has said it best.

> God does not intend that man shall have a place reserved for him to work in, since the true poverty of spirit requires

that man shall be emptied of God and all his works, so that if God wants to act in the soul, he himself must be in the place in which he acts.

This idea of true poverty is strange and difficult to understand in a world filled with work and wealth. To provide a room or space within so God can work might seem a bit strange in our postmodern world. Such poverty is not the result of sloth or laziness, drunkenness or a state in which a victim has no control, but rather voluntary poverty demonstrated by the poor widow in Mark 12:44. In a world where wealth is desired and strived for, poverty is seen as a virtue alongside severe ordeal of affliction and abundant joy. (See 2 Corinthians 8:2).

One Summer I went with three other men for a weekend at The Abbey of Gethsemane – a Trappist monastery located just south of Bardstown, Kentucky in the beautiful hills of Nelson County. This was to be a spiritual retreat – one of silence and reflection as guests of this Trappist community who held strictly to the 'vows' of silence. There was only two or three areas within and around the monastery where talking was permitted. We were also told that if we had any books to return them to our car, that they would only get in the way of our purpose of a spiritual retreat. This was asking a lot of four men who were from a city in which every minute was filled with talk or some kind of noise. This was especially difficult for one of the men who owned a business and had become an office of one. He spent most of his time in his van constantly going from one job to another or receiving calls for jobs and making estimates. He would even take his phone on vacation with him. Once I phoned Jack, forgetting he was in Florida on vacation with his family, and he answered poolside on his cell phone. Subsequently I asked Jack why he felt he always had to have his phone with him and felt so compelled to answer it. He quickly responded, "Because if I don't answer they will call my competitors." He went on to say an answering machine is of little value because people will not wait – they will simply hang up and call someone else. Jack might be a little more driven in this regard in that he and his family were almost homeless at one time seeking assistance from a charitable organization. He once told me. "Tom, I live in fear that I might become like that again."

cell phones in every place

never alone without a phone

the office is always open

an ever present god

in a highly competitive world

availability with furious competition

a necessity in suburbia

resting never while in travel or still

the coronary will wait

got to pay bills

to shut the office door

and drop my phones

is to be shot down

in the streets where business soars

and to know life no more

While at Gethsemane we would accuse Jack of making trips out to his van in the parking lot to call home and to receive messages from his cell phone. I don't think any of us really thought Jack would do this but we knew his compulsion in this regard and he was fun to kid because he took it so well. Out of the four of us, Jack seemed most to enjoy this time at Gethsemane and to really know the full value of our experience. While at Gethsemane we requested some time with one of the monks. This monk was an older man who had been at the monastery for a number of years and appeared to have much wisdom, which we hoped to tap into. We shared with this brother that we were from a big city unlike Gethsemane where the silence and way of being was so conducive to spiritual renewal. Chicago land was most demanding, calling us to work hard by staying on top of things in a complicated society and, in return, often feeling stressed as well as rewarded for our work. Most of us were successful, but at what cost? I will never forget this monk's response. First, he told us to find as much silence as possible. Furthermore, we need to realize that we know nothing and moreover, the monk asked that we remember that we are exactly where we need to be.

Silence is at a premium in the greater Chicago area as it is in most large cities and when this monk suggested that we find as much silence as possible we all looked at one another as if to say, "That's impossible in the world we live in." How can anyone have silence with a cell phone strapped to his or her belt? How can we have any silence when we are in an office twenty-four hours a day? This is a different world from Gethsemane. I can't help but think that even in the church complex in which I served as an associate pastor there is no silence. It is next to impossible to find a place where you are not interrupted in one fashion or another. The church has no chapel set aside for uninterrupted prayer or meditation. The whole space is used for study, worship, youth meetings and bands, choir practice, organ rehearsal and many, many other activities. These are good activities and ministries but where is there room for silence? I addressed this issue early with there being no holy place in the church, which goes hand in hand with this issue of the need for silence.

I have come to realize that this is the way it is in the dominant society in which we live – a society of activity, doing, accomplishing concrete things, filling space with noise whether it be singing, talking, playing an instrument or some other choice of noise making. How can we possibly hear from God when we fill our space with so much noise? I find this to be true with prayer as well. I find people are quick to pray but not so quick to listen. Has anyone heard from the Lord, is a question I often like to ask. I only get strange looks in response. Of course we don't hear from the Lord! How can we with so much noise going on! Then even if we did hear from the Lord would anyone be interested? Would we recognize the voice?

We might do well to take a lesson from the story about the call of Samuel in I Samuel 3. We read that it was a time when,"…the word of the Lord was rare…there was no frequent vision." (I Samuel 3:1b) As we read on we find how difficult it is for Samuel to hear God calling him even with the help of the priest, Eli. We might do well today to examine the various barriers that block our hearing of God's call. What is it that we put between us and the Lord that gets in our way of hearing God's call?

Thomas Merton tells us that silence is his salvation; a strange way to look at salvation and yet if we are to hear and respond to God we indeed must be silent. According to the Samuel story we also find that we need to have some expectation that God is trying to speak to us. Just perhaps there is little difference between the time in which Samuel lived and the living of our own days. What if we were to think half as much and become silent much more? Do we live in a world in which the word of the Lord is rare? Do you expect to hear anything from the Lord?

My father appeared to have a great respect and appreciation for the quiet, the simple and silence. I have known him to sit quietly for long periods of time almost in a meditative state. Perhaps for him it was a time to be reflective, or perhaps a time to stop reflecting and to just clear his mind of the business of the day. He would sit with his eyes closed and when I would ask if he was asleep, he always replied, "No, just resting my eyes."

Do you suppose we place too much importance on verbalization and activity when it comes to what we think is of high priority and of necessity? In the church the rising of funds for the budget was an annual grueling event. Stewardship season places emphasis on the giving of time, talent and money but I think almost everyone knew money to be of supreme importance. I was always amazed with the amount of money and energy spent on this activity. The preacher would often preach a series of sermons on stewardship or pay an expert fund raising preacher to provide this service. It was not unusual to contract with paid fundraisers to administer an elaborate fund raising program that would spread over a number of weeks.

A number of years ago a fellow pastor called me asking if I remembered all the time and energy we used to place on fund raising. Of course I had remembered, how could I have forgotten such moments in ministry, if indeed this can be called ministry. My friends went on saying, "No more. When stewardship season came around I just hand out slips of paper asking the members of the congregation to write on the paper what they think they can give financially for the upcoming year." He went on to explain that the slips of paper were collected from which the annual budget was comprised. My friend said the church never has failed to collect more money than the people said they could give. Why make things difficult? Why over do? Just bite off half as much and chew it twice as long.

I would add another dimension to my friend's stewardship program, which I would refer to as 'simple accountability and transparency.' I have found much concern in the church for a simple and easy manner in which to find answers to questions concerning how money is spent and what it is spent for. Too often an elaborate budget is made available which is just too complicated for many people to comprehend even after it has been explained. I suggest this process be given over to the church committees. That they place on a single page what was purchased, the amount and the ministry performed. Any member or friend of the church could easily see the workings of the church both financially and in ministry. Again we take small simple bites, chew long and reap benefits. After quiet reflection we can then not only make good decisions for our giving but feel good toward our congregation who wishes to simplify, practice transparency and demonstrate responsibility.

Our economy has hit an all time low except for the great depression, which has been contributed to greed. It has put many of us into a financial situation in which doing with a lot less is a necessity. Many individuals and families are now dependent upon community food banks and shelters resulting from unemployment and homes being reprocessed by the banking industry. These folk know what it's like to eat half as much with many eating even less than half. It appears the more we have the more we want regardless of how fat we become. My father went through the depression back in the thirties and he was always very aware of our resources valuing water, electricity and other accommodations to which we have become so accustomed. It seems being without makes one more appreciative and more able to conserve. I recall my father taking a bath in what must have been about six inches of water by the sound of the splashing about and the bones hitting porcelain. And when my brother and I would leave a light burning without using it, Dad would passionately say, 'You're burning my money'. When money and material things become so important it keeps us from being fully human and unable to back away from the table, eating half as much and chewing it twice as long.

The country of Denmark pays income tax of 50% to 60%, which enables them to provide health and education to all their citizens. When asked if this was not socialism they respond that it is not, but rather being human and showing love and care for all their people. Is this not a type of eating half as much? And is providing all this care not a type of chewing it twice as long?

LISTEN FOR YOUR NAME

Listen for your name
called from the deep,
called from the distance
shadows of the soul,
awakening the self from sleep.

Listen for your name
as a whisper from off the wind
questionable yet known
as if from a brush of an angel's wing,
a holy message sent.

Listen for your name
calling as Samuel slept,
disturbing, awakening,
waiting patiently
being adept.

NINE ELEVEN

Wealth enjoyed while
feeling invincible
as power abounds
in a hostile world.

Yet less secure
that we've been raped
exposing vulnerability.
Welcome to the world community.

Do we again seek instant gratification
or unity and rebirth?
Respect for one another
or fragment all the more?

Fear the ego that inflates.
Romance the shadow that runs deep.
Seek justice.
Love mercy.
Walk humbly with God.

The idols have ears but do not hear…

so unlike you, for all your hearing…

so like us, ears but do not hear.

Move us beyond ourselves, our favorite clichés,

our tired resentments,

our worn out habits,

to your newness.

Walter Brueggemann

NINE ELEVEN

I had the day off on September eleven and was at home working on the computer when Joy called to me saying, "Turn on the T.V.! Terrorists have just struck the World Trade Towers in New York!" Like most I sat in disbelief of what I was seeing on T.V. I guess I always knew this was a real possibility, and yet, to see with my own eyes one of our own commercial airlines fly into one of the World Trade Towers was shocking! More shocking was to see the panic, fear and desperation of the people as they began jumping out of windows.

One of the first images that came to me was that of neighbor. What kind of neighbor would do such a thing? Who would have so much hate toward this country that they would deliberately set out to murder thousands of innocent people on a bright clear day in one of the greatest cities in the world? What has happened to the global neighborhood? All three of the major monotheistic religions of the world hold to the belief of loving one's neighbor. All have a strong sense of showing hospitality. I quickly came to the conclusion that this act of terrorism had nothing to do with religion and everything to do with evil. If one is to talk about this of religion it can only be addressed as sick religion. We have seen such sick religion on a much lesser scale such as the Jonestown tragedy in November 1978. We need only look on the Internet under *Groups listed in Patterns of Global Terrorism, 2000* to find a long list of terrorist groups from Abu Nidal Organization (ANO) to Zviadists. Most of these groups and organizations are made up of individuals from countries that have oppressive governments or dictators who disallow the people a voice, leaving them angry and depressed. Such situations continue to exist and the more the people are oppressed the more they turn to desperate means, distorting and interpreting their religious faith to justify their terrorist ways.

While meeting with the Muslim community following nine eleven I found this same understanding with a Northwestern student from Syria who was of the Muslim faith. This student attributed political oppression and distortion of the faith to the nine eleven terrorist attacks. He went on to say that the United Nations Community does not help in that many countries of the world are not stable enough to have consistent leadership but are constantly being overthrown, therefore failing to have representation in the United Nations. People who do not have a voice due to repression will in turn become defiant, finding others who are of the same mindset and form cells or groups who will use any means to strike back.

For a number of years I had been teaching a course on evil in a large Presbyterian Church and the course was scheduled again just a few days following nine eleven. I found this to be a wonderful opportunity to challenge and encourage the students to do the same – to keep an open mind and spirit, as we looked at how this tragic event can speak to us as individuals, as a nation and as citizens of the global community. It is extremely difficult to examine oneself individually or collectively when under attack or wounded. It seems only natural to become defensive and, like a wounded animal, attack the very one that is trying to be of assistance. It was quite natural to unite behind our country as we sang God Bless America over and over while waving flags from our homes, vehicles and businesses. Yet we can wrap ourselves in the flag so tightly that we cut off our circulation and become blinded to our own dark side. The shadow side of ourselves should be explored for the benefit of growth and wholeness during such tragic moments, and yet we too often get in defense of the ego ideal while ignoring our shadow.

> The usual way that people try to deal with the problem of the shadow is simply to deny its existence. This is because awareness of one's shadow brings guilt and tension, and forces upon us a difficult psychological and spiritual task. On the other hand, denial of the shadow does not solve the problem but simply makes it worse. Not only do we then lose contact with the positive aspects of this dark side of ourselves, but we will also very likely project this dark side onto other people.[1]

When I was in psychotherapy I would bring dreams that didn't seem to be that important because they could so easily be interpreted and my analyst would say, "I don't want to hear those ego dreams, you know what they mean, give me dreams from your shadow."

So the case might be for nine eleven. We know of the pain and horror of it all and how damn angry it makes us and yet it's the unconscious, shadowy aspect of it all that we need to look at if we are to genuinely grow spiritually and emotionally as members of this global community. This is not to say that we should not grieve, indeed we should and must grieve, but then we need to move to a deeper level if we are to see the bigger picture and respond appropriately. Nor is this saying we should not hold accountable those who have done this horrible thing and to bring them to justice. Indeed we should and must, and yet we still need to move beyond, even bring these persons, cell groups and governments to justice. If we are to maximize the benefits of this experience we must not only be in defense of the ego ideal but also embrace the shadow lest we project it onto others and repeat or set up a scenario where it will happen again.

> A group, culture, or nation has a certain collective ego ideal, which in turn creates a collective Shadow. So the Nazis, with their collective ego ideal of Aryan superiority, had a corresponding collective Shadow. The United States, with the collective ego ideal of "Manifest Destiny" (the doctrine held by the United States in the nineteenth century that it was the white man's manifest destiny to possess the North American continent), created in turn a collective Shadow that was experienced by the Native American Indians, who were all but exterminated in a manner that was as ruthless and cruel as the Nazis' attempt to exterminate the Jews. Insofar as individuals within a group or nation become identical with the prevailing cultural consciousness, they too partake of the collective Shadow. It takes considerable individual consciousness to escape from such an identification, so that our individual shadow qualities, and the collective Shadow of our culture and time, inevitably become intermingled. 2

I especially like a comment from Walter Cronkite soon after the nine eleven tragedies when he was interviewed on one of the national networks saying, "I would hope that we would consider investing more in the Peace Corps". This gets at my initial response to nine eleven – what has happened to the neighborhood? I was even more reminded of this idea of neighborhood when I heard that the terrorists were told to live and operate out of neighborhoods where they could be most unnoticed. I understand they picked the American suburbs where most of us live and complain of not knowing our neighbor. All this reminded me of how much we have progressed in such a short time – or is it really progression?

162

The past is too close from radio to television

From the slow-way to the expressway

Porch swings are idol

While lazy-boys are saddled

Football the idol

Malls become weekend sanctuaries

The past is too close.

So much has transpired in such a short time, leaving a taste in our mouths for something that has been left behind – the past is too close. A hunger for something that is very basic in life has left us rather bored and indifferent to the abundance that has sped up life to the point that we have left in the dust that which grounds us and gives meaning and purpose to daily living. There is a hunger in our country for more than wealth, professional success often playing itself out as wealth, and for bigger toys for which we can better entertain ourselves. Our security is in all the wrong places, which is especially demonstrated first by Ronald Reagan and by George Bush number two. It is the thinking of these presidents, as well as many American citizens, that our national security is based on might and power acquired through military technology. This thinking is most prevalent in the Star Wars idea of Reagan and which continued to be realized through the Bush administration. This thinking is isolationism at its best, or worst. It is arrogant and egocentric assuming we are God and most capable of saving ourselves from a hostile world through our technological resources. Naipaul says it well, "...the more protective the bubble in which one lives, the more uncertain one's knowledge becomes of what lies out there". 3

The taste in our mouths that we are unable to identify, that taste that we keep trying to satisfy through our own hard work and technological savvy, is nothing more than a taste for spiritual food that cannot be acquired through wealth or highly developed minds that trust in that which does not make for peace.

> Hunger abounds
>
> While eating is all around
>
> Appetites grow
>
> Materialism soars
>
> Porch swings idol
>
> Impotence known
>
> With viagara for passion
>
> Yet hunger abounds
>
> While eating in all the wrong places

On an international level we need more porches and rocking chairs where we can sit a spell, getting to know and appreciate one another on a much deeper level. We need a place and time to come to the realization that we are all most valuable and that as long as we remain a threat to one another we contribute only to the misery of the world particularly to the innocent. We need to discuss that security and peace are not in bombs, missile shields and bigger and better military technology, but rather in how we can better uplift one another as brothers and sisters of the world. We need to invest in loving our neighbors, not in controlling them with power and might. Walter Cronkite is right when he states that we need to invest more in our Peace Corps. The Peace Corps is a great way of sharing our technology in a loving positive manner – lifting up nations that are less resourceful. This would be a wonderful way to love our neighbors. This would be one of the best ways to provide real security among the people of the world. Whenever we are investing in the poor through feeding the hungry, building homes or upgrading their educational skill we are securing peace in a potentially hostile situation. It would also be helpful for us as a powerful and resource nation to look carefully at what we need or could possibly learn from the disadvantaged and poor. No one wants to be seen as all needy without anything to offer others. America could perhaps be challenged to see how we might benefit from the less fortunate and seek to build healthy relationships based on our mutual skills and talents as a particularly gifted people of the world. D.H. Lawrence, in his poem, "To be alive you've got to feel a generous flow", says it well.

> The only reason for living is being fully alive; and you can't be fully alive if you are crushed by secret fear, and bullied with the threat – get money or eat dirt! – and forced to do a thousand mean things, meaner than your nature, and forced to clutch on to possessions in the hope they'll make you feel safe, and forced to watch everyone that comes near you lest they've come to do you down.

> Without a bit of common trust in one another, we can't live. In the end, we go insane. It is the penalty of fear and meanness, being meaner than our natures.

> To be alive, you've got to feel a generous flow, and under a competitive system that is impossible, really. The world is waiting for a great new movement of generosity, or for a great wave of death. We must change the system, and make living free to all men, or we must see men die; and then die ourselves.4

The Christmas following nine eleven took on a special meaning for me especially as it is recorded in the second chapter of Matthew concerning the slaughter of the innocents in Bethlehem. The killing of the innocent boys age two and under by Herod and the flight to Egypt by Joseph and Mary with the Divine Child is Matthew's way of bridging between the old salvation stories and prophecies, and the new salvation event in Jesus, and yet there are many applications to our own lives. None of us can stay in Bethlehem for long, nor should we, no more than we can stay in the Garden of Eden, a place of the innocent – a preconscious state of awareness where everything is experienced as it happens without fear of anticipation. There is absolutely no potential for spiritual growth in Bethlehem – it is only a beginning place – a birthing place for our journey to spiritual maturity. We must be dispersed, or rejected that we might experience the dawning of moral consciousness – our awareness of our genuine calling as the people of God. As we move from Bethlehem we lose our innocent state as seen in the Archetype, Innocence, where one remains in service to the ego – being 'puffed up'; and living in a state equivalent to the maternal womb. This innocence is represented by Adam and Eve before the 'fall,' and by Moses, as a baby, being rescued by the daughter of a hostile Pharaoh who demanded the death of all newborn Hebrew infants to protect his throne, and by the patriarch, Joseph, who was favored by his father, Jacob, over his brothers. All of these Biblical characters, including Jesus, were called into Egypt from the Innocent Archetype to take on the Orphan Archetype to save their people. In these Biblical characters we find the innocent forced into homelessness. Like Israel of old, Jesus must discover himself through wandering which is the positive work of the orphan. The orphan is the state in which we find ourselves after the fall or in flight to Egypt. This can be a prolonged journey to maturity if we seek only to return to our innocent state through denial or defensiveness. As much as we long for Eden or Bethlehem it's not there. As much as we long to rid our lives of Herods, Pharaohs or Bin Ladens they will always be with us.

I have heard many people say their lives will never be the same since nine eleven. Is this a move from innocent to orphan? Have we as Americans been in an innocent state? My daughter called me up that morning of nine eleven crying and saying, "Dad, I have never known or experienced anything like this in my lifetime". Were we placed in a helpless state, vulnerable, unsafe and afraid for the first time in this strong nation of ours? An older gentleman said to me shortly after nine eleven, "I think we all thought we were invincible." In a sense this is like being moved from Innocent to Orphan. In the orphan state we have the opportunity to move on, evolving to a healthier and a more faithful state, if we don't seek to blame others, pout and look for new caretakers enabling us to remain in this orphan state.

If we are to move beyond this orphan state I think there are at least three things we should become more aware of: 1) Listen to God. Ever notice how quick people are to pray but how few of us listen? Do you know anyone who has heard from the Lord lately? God spoke to Joseph and allowed the family to move to safety. Pay attention to your dreams, for this is how God chose to speak in the Scriptures. God communicates with us through our unconscious, not during our waking moments, at least most of the time. 2) When all is going well remember that no one can stay in Bethlehem forever. 3) When bad things happen it could be for a purpose, acting as a catalyst to help us get to the place we need to be.

Perhaps nine eleven was a catalyst to move us from a state of complacency or indifference, which might be another way of defining the Innocent/Orphan Archetype. Matthew Fox in his most recent book uses the word *acedia* to refer to misdirected love or arrogance to describe America's number one sin.

> Etymologically the word *acedia* is said to have two derivatives. One is *a-kedos* in Greek, which means "not caring." The other is from the word for *sour*. There is a not-caring aspect to acedia, a lack of passion, and there is also an attitude of sourness or cynicism toward life. It is said that acedia "consists in loving a great good with less intensity than it deserves; it is 'slow love.' 'Slow love' is Dante's definition for acedia. A 'slow love' is presumably love that fails to connect to the cosmic love.

> The opposite of acedia is *joy*, a joy at spiritual things. A joyless culture is a culture locked in acedia.

> I believe that acedia is the most dominant sin of our

culture today. Couch-potato-itis is a conspiracy (conscious or unconscious) of an economic system that is geared to rendering consumerism a daily addiction. Our economic system creates a kind of spiritual enslavement.5

If Matthew Fox is correct in his assessment of America it might well explain why depression is on the rise with more people taking anti-depression and anti-anxiety medication since nine eleven. Alcohol consumption is also on the rise, which is only another drug of choice. In an article by John Navone entitled "Spiritual Acedia, Torpor and Depression" we read, "Acedia, depression, steals life away. It immobilizes us because it robs us of the hope we need to believe something good is possible. It deadens our belief in God's love and goodness." Too many in our country are sad, bored and joyless and are looking for solutions through drugs or entertainment rather than getting in dialogue with others to discuss our sad attitude that is eating away at our souls. The church has become a major part of the problem by failing to address this issue of *acedia*. For the most part the church has played into the despair and sadness of our culture to keep people happy, the pews filled, and the offerings up to pay for the high cost of religion today. As a Pastoral Counselor and Marriage and Family Therapist I find that most people do not want to deal with the real issues behind their depression or anxiety but only to be given a drug for a quick and easy way out. We will do anything to remain in Bethlehem rather than to move on to our Egypt and beyond as God's heroic people.

Where Matthew Fox uses the Greek term *acedia* to describe our present American culture, James Hillman, psychologist, scholar, international lecturer and author writes about this issue through a thorough examination of the soul or what he would rather call the acorn theory. Hillman's study takes us on a search of character and calling. Hillman speaks candidly and honestly at the end of his book about "American mediocrity".

We must also admit, despite our previous judgment against mediocrity as a psychologically valid term, that we have uncovered the psychological condition that generates American mediocrity. The capacity to deny, to remain innocent, to use belief as a protection against sophistications of every sort – intellectual, aesthetic, moral, psychological – keeps the American character from awakening. The American character remains blind to the fact that the virtues of mediocrity – those pieties of disciplined energy, order, self-control, probity, and faith – are themselves messengers of the devil they would overcome.6

Hillman comes to the conclusion that the common denominator is the invincibility of belief. Examples can be Ollie North and George W. Bush for their lies and yet their strong belief in America "…allowed them to go forward uncorrupted in the midst of dirty doings, untouched by their own shadows, innocent". 7 Hillman goes on to say that it is this American habit of belief that appeals to our Main Street mediocrity.

Hillman also challenges the reader to take a good look at his own personal involvement in this societal loss of soul, loss of daemonic inspiration or loss of character.

Maybe inviting mediocrity in – just doing a passable job as a team player, not upsetting the boat, holding on to "family values," joining the Walmart community, staying cool, fearing extremists and ungrounded underground ideas – is precisely what drives the invisible away. Let us not forget that societies are elevated and rewarded by those who are inspired: the emergency nurse; the teacher of the year; the basketball guard who arcs a perfect three-pointer. The inspired moment does not invalidate the team, but belongs to the context of the team and to its wider home town public. To sink the shot in the final second and thereby save a crucial game is not merely an isolated heroic act. It reconstitutes the hero itself within an archetypal context: The hero is the one who performs inspired deeds for the glory of the city and its gods. Our civilizations, egocentric competitive notions of inspired actions makes us miss their societal service. "Inspiration" means simply "in – breathing of spirit," not "exaltation of the spirited."8

No one knows this better than the Appalachian whose land has been raped of its coal and oil by the big corporations of this country: Corporate America who came into the Appalachian Mountains giving praise to the uneducated citizens for their food and hospitality while, all the time, setting them up to sign "broad-form deeds," giving all mineral rights to these corporations. Taking the coal was not enough in that such corporations set up coal camps where miners and their families lived in poverty – enslaved to the big coal companies. We hear the voice of Tennessee Ernie Ford singing, "I Sold My Soul To The Company Store"; but this was only the beginning.

> At a time of recent economic boom, many Kentuckians do not share in the state's economic prosperity. Kentucky continues to tax working people back into poverty. The report, **State Income Tax Burdens on Low-Income Families in 2000: Assessing the Burden and Opportunities for Relief** notes that "More than a decade ago, the federal government recognized the inconsistency of encouraging poor families to work and then levying taxes that pushed them deeper into poverty. President Ronald Reagan spoke forcefully in the mid 1980's about the foolishness of taxing poor households deeper into poverty. Many states have made progress, but 19 states, including Kentucky, still levy income taxes on two parent families of four with earnings below the poverty level.9

According to the U.S Health and Human Services the poverty threshold is $22,050 for a family of four living in the contiguous states and D.C. In Kentucky families of four are taxed at $20,700, which is well below the poverty line. (Federal Register, Vol. 74, No 14, January 23, 2009, pages 4199-4201)

It is my perception that the folk in Appalachia don't put

much energy into "growing up"; not the type of growing up that we usually think of when we use this term but rather just the opposite – a sense of growing down. A sense of being rooted with feet firmly planted on the ground. When one grows down there is no need to concur or to become superior over another but rather to feel comfortable right where life happens to place you.

> Organ images of growth follow the favorite symbol for human life, the tree, but I am turning that tree up side down. My model of growth has its roots in heaven and imagines a gradual descent downward toward human affairs. This is the Tree of the Kabbalah in the Jewish and also Christian mystical tradition. The Zohar, the main Kabbalist book, makes it clear that the descent is tough; the soul is reluctant to come down and get messed by the world.10

I'm not for a minute thinking that all Appalachia folk are like this but I am saying that this fits my father to a tee – unafraid to get dirty, making friends with the poor and friendless and to never feel he was ever better than anyone else. My father had the advantage over many people who 'grew up,' for Dad was always "growing down" therefore not having to struggle with that long fall, to *really* get on his feet. I have heard that there is a real connection between the two words *soul* and *sole* – more than just that they sound alike. Just perhaps we get *soul* through our *soles* from the good earth in which we were created. Who goes without shoes with *soles* to the earth but the poor, those who have been growing down.

America has a long history of treating people unfairly and even criminally under the disguise of patriotism or religion. When a commentator reported about no weapons of mass destruction being found in Iraq, he suggested the president had misled the American people. When questioning President George W. Bush about this matter, Mr Bush quickly responded, "I did what was best for the American people." End of discussion. Evidence of the misleading power of belief is seen in the Bush administration stating, if you fail to believe as we do then you are unpatriotic.

How difficult it is to have character and be genuinely called in the midst of this American habit of belief. Are we any different from the children of Israel who at one point only wanted to return to slavery under an abusive Egyptian government, the dominate culture, rather than be awakened from out of mediocrity?

I suspect the Appalachian poor have a better understanding of what happened on nine eleven than any one in the Bush administration. It was no mistake that the world trade center located in the most prestigious city in the wealthiest country in the world was brutally attacked by terrorists who felt powerless; Arab terrorists who strongly felt that the United States had treaded too deep into their culture; Arab terrorists who felt that their own government had sold out to the imperial Americans; Arab terrorists who felt that their oil was more important than the people of the Middle East. The Appalachian poor know what it is to be so abused by those who are 'growing up.' Those who are 'growing up' are the egocentric who are only looking to capitalize for their own gain and will go to any extent to get what they want. 'Growing down' is to move from a single-minded egocentricity into a common humanity, which I most clearly see in my Appalachian father.

I end this chapter with another quote from James Hillman who in many ways has a wonderful response to nine-eleven though it was written a few years before the nine-eleven tragedy, and even more tragic response from the Bush administration.

> For adequate rituals we substitute rigidities and formulaic fixes like "three strikes and you're out. "Without exorcisms that attempt to separate the Devil and the daemon, we have only eradications that get rid of both. Rituals not only protect society from the demonic; they

also protect it from its own paranoia, from falling prey to its own obsessive and vicious measures of purification, that ever-present American myth: the return to innocence in a Puritan paradise. 11

I remember so well my days as a student at Louisville Presbyterian Theological Seminary when America was experiencing both the horrors of the Vietnam War and the evils of racism. Those were days filled with high emotions and opinions. Days when action seemed to be called for even though many times it seemed only to make things more confusing. A sign hung outside the office of Sam Keen reading "We need chairs." Many thought this was crazy and yet Sam Keen knew the value of sitting a spell when all else was going to hell.

If we were to discuss nine eleven and its aftermath today I would hope it would reflect some learning. Did the U.S. go after the terrorists that attacked us on Nine eleven? I don't think so. Can we fight terrorists like we would fight a conventional war? I don't think so. I would hope such discussion would look at how we are fighting a ghost war, one in which the enemy is almost impossible to identify. An enemy that in all likelihood is in a proxy war for other nations. Did not Iran pay the Hezbollah, soldiers of God, to defeat Israel in Lebanon in 2000? I suspect powerful nations can no longer defeat others by conventional warfare. Who would have thought Muslim guerrilla forces could and did defeat the heavy armor of Russia? We often like to see things as black or white and respond accordingly when there are all shades involved. I suspect where we might see terrorist groups as nothing but evil, others benefit from their presence and terroristic activity. The more I reflect upon our military activities in the Middle East the more I respect and admire the statement by Walter Cronkite, following nine-eleven, "I would hope that we would consider investing more in the Peace Corps."

It appears the United States continues to believe it can get its way through materialism, with its highly sophisticated armies and weaponries. I think it is clearly evident that this is not the manner in which we should be living in the global neighborhood. I would suggest we follow the way of Greg Mortenson, author of the best selling book entitled *Three Cups of Tea*. After failing in his attempt to climb K2 (world's second highest mountain) and being rescued by the people of a Pakistan village, Montenson began a peacemaking mission. This mission came only after listening to the people, being moved by the inhabitants' kindness and opening his heart to their needs. On the back cover of Mortenson's book we read a statement by Haji Ali, Korphe Village Chief, Karakoram Mountains, Pakistan. "Here (in Pakistan and Afghanistan), we drink three cups of tea to do business, the first you are a stranger, the second you become a friend, and the third, you join our family, and for family we are prepared to do anything – even die."

Just perhaps as a country we need to learn how to drink tea. How to respond to a peoples' graciousness, become friends, listen and respond with compassion. Yes, there are terrorists in Afghanistan and Pakistan but just perhaps we get to the terrorist first by befriending the people, drinking the three cups of tea, becoming family and then together terrorism might be more easily over come. I think it's a matter of learning how to live peaceably in the global neighborhood.

The compassionate activity by Greg Mortenson's Central Asia Institute has built more than eighty schools in the remote regions of Pakistan and Afghanistan. The *Wall Street Journal,* December 26, 2008, has Mortenson saying, "...that the cost of a Tomahawk cruise missile ($840,000) would be better spent building dozens of schools instead."

The United States has its war institutes such as Air Force Academy, West Point, Naval Academy and others that train some of our finest men and women for war. I have often wondered why our country does not invest in a peace academy to prepare an equal amount of our fine men and women for a mission of peace at home and around the world. Just think of how wonderful it would be to have U.S. peacemakers around the world building houses and schools, digging wells and teaching children. I think the benefits would be enormous!

The Christian Century, published an article entitled <u>Another Kind of Surge</u> supporting the work that Greg Mortenson is doing in Afghanistan. The article goes on to say how Afghanistan needs an infusion of development, not a surge of troops. In early December, as President Obama was announcing that he was sending 30,000 more troops to Afghanistan, Greg Mortenson was releasing his book *Stones into Schools,* as a follow-up to his 2006 best seller *Three Cups of Tea.* Mortenson has logged more months in remote parts of Afghanistan and Pakistan than almost any other Westerner. He has forged relationships with the tribal leaders in an effort to learn what they want. Often what they want is a village school.

It is encouraging that Obama and top military leaders understand the importance of working with local leaders to create schools, clinics and economic opportunities. But armed with that knowledge, they should be launching a surge in development, not a surge in troops. Instead of deploying 30,000 more soldiers, the U.S. would be better off deploying 30,000 more Greg Mortensons.

The Christian Century, December 29, 2009

INNOCENCE TO ORPHAN
AND BEYOND

At home in the village,
comfort abounding,
tall buildings in the landscape,
country cottage for retreat with
warm fires inviting.

Buildings fall
exposing innocence,
left naked among the rubble.
Expeditiously removed from
edenic bliss –
Anger rages.

Nakedness covered
with garments of the gods,
victims all –
paradise lost,
forced to be an orphan.

Let the heroic journey begin
from Egypt to promised land
with courage to seek who we really are,
wandering with purpose
pilgrims of deep faith.

WHAT IS PRAYER?

What is prayer?
But to experience the full essence of life
Exploring the joys of living
Diving into the depths of pain
Knowing that life is real

What is prayer?
But to express with passion
Rage toward injustice
Compassion for the poor
And yet walk humbly with God

What is prayer?
But to cry with those who cry
Laugh with those who laugh
To know the difference

What is prayer?
If not to be angered with war
To love one's enemy
To question God
Yet praise him above all

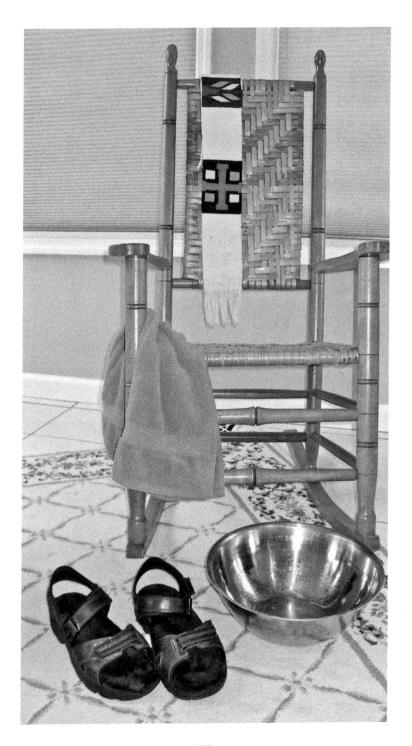

A prayer makes sense only if it is lived. Unless it is "lived", unless life and prayer become completely interwoven, prayer becomes a sort of polite madrigal, which you offer God at moments when you are giving time to Him.

Anthony Bloom

All the world is queer except me and thee, and sometimes I think thee is a little queerer.

The Quakers

The opposite of good is not evil, it is indifference.

Abraham Joshua Heschel

The Full Essence of Life

My father was not one to drink alcoholic drinks except on rare occasions. Yet he would often enjoy talking about various uses of corn both as a food and as a drink. I have heard him laugh and say, "I like my bourbon straight to get the full essence of the corn". On other occasions he might talk of how he liked his coffee black to enjoy the full essence of the bean. Dad enjoyed the full essence of life – life as something to be savored, sacred and holy. Life is not to be polluted. I don't think anyone enjoyed life more than my father, fully emerging himself in living, never taking anything for granted and knowing that it had nothing to do with material wealth.

The poem, "What is prayer?" that introduced this chapter was written for a Lenten service in 2003 for a congregation in Arlington Heights, Illinois. Unknowingly or unconsciously, I wrote a prayer that could have easily been written by my father. After I thought about it I was not at all surprised in that my father has so heavily influenced me. Of the services for this Lenten season planned around the subjects of prayer, my pick was 'Living as Prayer.'

Prayer and spiritual intimacy are not things we pull aside to do, but rather are a way of life to be lived. Indeed, life is prayer, a living communion with a relationship. Prayer is the very essence of life. Essence is the most important ingredient, the crucial element in the very nature of life.

The best examples can be found in the Scriptures. In John 12:1-8 we have the story of Mary, sister of Martha and Lazarus, washing the feet of Jesus with costly perfume. Letting her hair fall from a tightly wrapped bun, she wiped from his feet the tears that were flowing from her compassionate and grieving face. In this moment of spontaneous outpouring love, the Gospel of Luke reports that she wet his feet with her tears, wiped his feet with her hair, kissed his feet, and then anointed his feet with the expensive perfume. Essence is to show an abundance of a quality and in this case it was the essence of love Mary showed to Jesus. It is of importance to note that in Webster's New World Dictionary essence is also defined as a perfume or scent.

This story of Mary washing Jesus' feet shows the essence of love in a spontaneous manner demonstrating prayer at the deepest level.

Experiencing the full essence of life

Exploring the joys of living

Diving into the depths of pain

Knowing that life is real

Judas raised the protest, "Why was this perfume not sold for three hundred denarii and the money given to the poor?" How easy to be critical of the spirituality (prayer) of others especially when your own is weak! Judas is a man with a good cause, but with evil behind it. John adds parenthetically: "This he said, not that he cared for the poor but because he was a thief, and as he had the money box he used to take what was put into it" (verse. 6). Here Judas wants to pollute the very essence of love that Mary was living out in the moment.

Prayer, at the very essence of life, continues to be demonstrated by Mary in another story found in Luke 10. In this story Mary again is able to determine the need of Jesus and provide the very essence of love that is called for by Jesus.

.... Martha was distracted by her many tasks, so she came to him and asked, "Lord do you not care that my sister has left me to do all the work by myself? Tell her then to help me." But the Lord answered her, "Martha, Martha, you are worried and distracted by many things; Mary has chosen the better part, which will not be taken away from her."

Luke 10:40-42

This story reinforces the whole idea of "sitting a spell" – of our being able to get out of the way and just be with the other who needs our undivided attention. Sometimes this is more important than all our busy activity. Too often our listening only becomes a time to formulate in our own minds how we are going to respond which keeps us from really listening to what another is saying. Jesus obviously realized that Mary was listening which might well be considered the essence of love and therefore genuine prayer.

Listen he would say

You learn more this way

With great zeal he would report

A tale, a word, a statement

Inviting a listening experience of sort

To experience prayer as the full essence of life is to be enraged by injustice in the world. The gospels portray Jesus as a man of compassion for the poor. We have only to look to those whom Jesus blessed to determine those for whom he had compassion – the poor, the hungry, those who grieve and those who are hated for taking Jesus seriously. We have only to look at the woes to determine those who angered Jesus – the rich, the full, those who laugh but should be in mourning. The Sermon on the Plain (Luke 6:17-49) directs us in our prayer life if we will only allow it to do so, not just in words but also in action – a style of life that demonstrates our understanding of "living as prayer."

> In the Prayer of Suffering we leave far behind our needs and wants, even our transformation and union with God. Here we give to God the various difficulties and trials that we face, asking him to use them redemptively. We also voluntarily take unto ourselves the griefs and sorrows of others in order to set them free. In our suffering those who suffer come to see the face of the suffering God. Joy, not misery, is the compelling energy behind redemptive suffering.1

What is prayer

But to express with passion

Rage toward injustice

Compassion for the poor

And yet walk humbly with God

To be in prayer is to be in grief for the world. Too often we laugh with those who cry and cry with those who laugh rather than to grieve and laugh appropriately. Prayer is to know the difference and to make a difference in a world that is indifferent. One of many examples is the attitude taken toward our "enemy" in Iraq and other places around the world. To have Iraqi prisoners strip naked and wear women's underwear over their heads is totally the opposite of understanding the full essence of life and to lead any kind of prayerful lifestyle. Such behavior is the very work of evil in the world and can only turn the countries and governments of the world more increasingly against the United States of America. War is not the way to peace; peace is the way to peace.

> If you love those who love you, what credit is that to you? For even sinners love those who love them. If you do good to those who do good to you, what credit is that to you? For even sinners do the same. If you lend to those from whom you hope to receive, what credit is that to you? Even sinners lend to sinners, to receive as much gain. But love your enemy, do good, and lend, expecting nothing in return. (Luke 6:32-35a)

This Scripture is of course impossible to live up to. Jesus gave us a hard message and yet perhaps it's that which we should at least strive toward. A real aspect of prayer is anger about the imperial warring attitude of our country. Not to be angry is to be both unpatriotic and people of little faith. Not to question our country and God is to become passive and indifferent as citizens, and to fail to engage God who sometimes appears to be disengaging and uncaring. This would be in keeping both with the Old Testament prophets and Jesus according to the Gospel writers.

What is prayer

But to cry with those who cry

Laugh with those who laugh

To know the difference

To make a difference

Yet when we talk about prayer, faith or the full essence of life there is a much bigger issue. The western world has been experiencing a great schism that has polarized its people into two distinct orientations – fundamentalism and secularism. These words, fundamentalism and secularism, might be too strong and carry too much of a connotation for many of us to identify with, however I suspect all of us lean toward one or the other to various degrees. Such orientations have long roots back to Descartes, Hobbes, Nietzsche and many others who view God as dead or at least retreating from the world. Sartre encouraged the rejection of God – a God who only restricts our freedom. "The existential world, which seems so exciting to a liberal, seems Godless, drained of meaning, and even satanic to a fundamentalist."2

This is true not only in the United States but also just as true in Israel where Hasidism (spirituals holding to the fundamental beliefs of the Torah) opposed the Zionists (Secularist Jews) who were behind the establishment of the nation of Israel. Hasidism believed Israel would be restored only with the coming of the Messiah. In other parts of the Middle East Muslims have always seen secularism as any attempt to destroy Islam.

> …it is important to recognize that these theologies and ideologies are rooted in fear. It is impossible to reason such fear away or attempt to eradicate it by coercive measures. A more imaginative response would be to try to appreciate the depth of this neurosis, even if a liberal or a secularist cannot share this dread-ridden perspective.3

Regardless of the nation or the spiritual belief this struggle continues to intensify among the people. Karen Armstrong brilliantly tells of the history of such fundamentalism in the United States beginning in the 60's with a permissive youth culture, the sexual revolution, the promotion of equal rights for women, blacks and homosexuals. It was not until the 70's that fundamentalism became offensive with Pat Robertson and Jerry Falwell who were determined to fight the human secularist and establish a separate society for "born again" Christians based on the literal interpretation of the scriptures.

Today in the world there is much anger and suspicion toward government that tries to impose this modernity or liberal ways upon the fundamentalist. In the United States fundamentalism and liberalism have become politicized to the point that candidates are identified and endorsed by one side or the other. The most clearly identified issues involve abortion and homosexuality. During the 2004 presidential election these issues came before the American people as related to the right and left political/religious perspectives, with pressure being felt by both religious groups and politicians. Senator John Kerry was obviously feeling this pressure.

Kerry gains cover with Catholics

May 3, 2004

By Robert Novak

Sun-Times Columnist

Readers of the Catholic Standard, official publication of the Archdiocese of Washington, D.C., raised their eyebrows upon learning of a 45-minute meeting April 15 of Sen. John Kerry with the Archbishop of Washington, Cardinal Theodore McCarrick. Why did Sen. Kerry seek a meeting with a prelate who was not his bishop and whom he had never met? The answer was grounded in high-level political intrigue. McCarrick Heads the task force on Catholic Participation in public life established by the U.S. bishops. Its most publicized task is to inquire whether politicians who defy Catholic teaching should receive the sacraments. About to become the first Catholic since John F. Kennedy to be nominated for president, Kerry was lobbying McCarrick against being denied Holy Communion as an unwavering pro-choice abortion advocate. Whether his lobbying helped, Kerry could not have been more pleased by his interview published in last

Thursday's Catholic Standard. While asserting abortion "may be primary," he added that "people who are with us on one issue" may be "against us on many other issues." McCarrick concluded:

"All these things will have to be weighed very carefully." Intentionally or not, he was following the lead of liberal, pro-choice Democrats and providing cover for Kerry with traditional Catholics.

The pro-choice politicians seem to be winning the first round, but a priest familiar with how the church operates told me that more and more American bishops, influenced by John Paul II, will deny communion and "finally 'out' liberal Catholics for what they are at heart, Protestants." This priest sees the day when "pro-abortion politicians will stop calling themselves Catholics or repent of their sin." That surely will not happen before the 2004 election.

Normally we think of Protestants as the fundamentalists and not Catholics, however fundamental beliefs are just that, whether they are derived from a literal interpretation of the Scriptures or handed down from a hierarchy with its leadership in Rome. Where Kerry visits the Archbishop of Washington, President Bush would visit Bob Jones University. Both are out to appease the fundamentalist association with these individuals or institutions to win over a large number of people who hopefully will vote for them come November.

Where is the normal American in all this division established by these two orientations of fundamentalism and secularism? I have found most to be totally turned off and withdrawn into their work, family and church or that activity that gives them pleasure or some sense of hope, which might be the church or a hunting or golf club. Most do not vote. In Kentucky recently an election was held for local officials and only 14% voted. I have found most of these folk have little hope in the political process. They don't read newspapers nor do they listen to the news. For the most part they are in denial and often get angry if politically engaged in any way.

I recently met a wonderfully respectful man who had been in the gospel ministry but dropped out and has now taken up carpentry and furniture making as a trade and livelihood. Sounds almost like a man in Galilee who lived some 2000 years ago. As we talked I found that he and his wife have six children ranging from ages two to twelve. He and his wife home school the children and they have no relationship with an organized church. He went on to share with me that organized schools and churches were not good for children and were teaching them the wrong things. He and his wife have little contact with the community except for a few friends with whom they "worship" on occasion.

I know a young woman in Chicago who has a high paying job who never feels secure, but is vulnerable in our economy with so much out sourcing to other countries. She is not married but lives with a man who shares her ideals and beliefs. They attend a big mega church where they don't have to identify themselves nor does anyone ask them to give money. The preacher makes them feel good with his sermons and the music is modern gospel, which leaves them feeling uplifted. They say other churches are boring and they leave feeling sad and depressed especially if they are always talking about social issues.

Where is that place where we can find the full essence of life? Is there a place where we can be about prayer? How do we go about finding this place? Do we have to be with those who think and act as we do? Are our lives so secular that the sacred has been squeezed out? Are our lives so filled with rage over modernity that we have lost all sense of compassion for others? Do you find the full essence of life in what you believe and the kind of life you live?

Is it necessary to withdraw from the world to be about prayer – to live our lives in love and peace for others? Is it just as easy to move in the other direction and immerse our lives into the secular world? Is life always about being politically correct or spiritually correct? Is life always about winning or losing?

> A great Rabbi died and left his spiritual work to his son to carry on. The son was a great man in his own right, but he did the work of a Rabbi in a completely different manner than his father. The people who had become used to the father's ways came to the son. "You are not doing what your father did," they complained. The son replied, "But indeed I am. He imitated no one and I am imitating no one".4

I wish my father was still alive so I could ask him what he thought of all this and yet I know what he would say. "Tom, everyone is peculiar, some are just more peculiar than others." Just perhaps the full essence of life is living up to our peculiarity with no apology.

I have come to find much meaning and therapeutic value in contemplative prayer. A prayer not so much about "method" or "system" than about being open, attentive with expectation and trust. Much like Eastern meditation, contemplative prayer is about being silent with concentration on one's breathing. I find it to be very much a natural state of being in the moment or the present. This prayer is not attempting to make any changes but rather to accept one's feelings, putting aside thoughts as they emerge. We often race away with our thoughts and as we do so they are exaggerated and only cause much stress and therefore we overreact or respond inappropriately. Contemplative prayer allows us to have realistic expectations based on who we are and what we are feeling in the moment. Thomas Merton says it well.

> Far from establishing one in unassailable narcissistic security, the way of prayer brings us face to face with the sham and indignity of the false self that seeks to live for itself alone and to enjoy the "consolation of prayer" for its own sake. This "self" is pure illusion, and ultimately he who lives for and by such an illusion must end either in disgust or in madness. 5

I have found contemplative prayer to enable grounding when I find thoughts to be racing away in my mind. Many people give up on this type of prayer or meditation too quickly feeling the flood of thoughts to be getting in the way. It is only after months and years of this type of prayer that we realize it's benefits, a time when thoughts are less and we become more comfortable just being in the moment rather than thinking and planning things over which we have no control. Contemplative prayer helps us to become more aware of just how much we live out of our heads seeking an intellectual solution to any difficulty or problem we might have. Where our thinking process makes things worse allowing only fabrication, projection and fantasy. Ego or our illusory sense of self disallows us to experience the full essence of life (prayer).

> All that is required to become free of the ego is to be aware of it, since awareness and ego are incompatible. Awareness is the power that is concealed within the present moment. This way we may also call it Presence. The ultimate purpose of human existence, which is to say, your purpose, is to bring that power into the world. And this is also why becoming free of the ego cannot be made into a goal to be attained at some point in the future. Only Presence can free you of the ego, and you can only be present now, not yesterday or tomorrow. Only Presence can undo the past in you and thus transform your state of consciousness. 6

A psychologist friend who is also a marriage and family therapist shared with me that over the years she has tried all the various therapeutic techniques and has found none to be as effective as Asia Meditation. She begins all her therapy groups with fifteen minutes of meditation allowing everyone to become centered into the present moment.

Just perhaps more and more people will learn that it is possible to "heal thy self" by taking the time to be silent and to allow the self to be in the present moment. I think we are more and more learning the value of silent meditation and are becoming more capable of applying it to our daily lives. However, meditation requires patience and persistence. Learning the technique and practicing it at least daily over a period of one year is necessary before feeling the full healing effect. Some will embrace meditation from a spiritual or even religious perspective while others will see it as science. I think our orientation toward meditation makes little difference. What is important is its daily practice. I take it as a prayer form and a supplement to my Christian faith. Most importantly I find meditation as a means of experiencing the full essence of life.

CIRCLE OF LIFE

Within the circle of life
A common base
Providing spiritual space
The power of mystery
Questioned never

Within the circle of life
Came the season of reason
It was with faith's fate
That life lost its sight
Now there's a fight

Within the circle of life
Evolved into the heavens
To find the throne empty
Void for the seculars
Sitting in comfort

Within the circle of life
Fundamentals reclaimed
Tolerance, inclusiveness, compassion neglected
Cultivating rage, resentment, revenge
Views demanded

Within the circle of life
Find a better way
Be not threatened
Just sit a spell
The holy beckons

BREATH

I listen to my breath filling my lungs
voluntarily, as if a life of its own lifts my
chest one moment while collapsing it the
next. Breath continues while I sleep, given
at birth, taken away at death –
    given, taken away,
        given, taken away,
like the ocean tide moving in only
to quickly move out, as if the earth
were breathing while the moon smiles
above, contracting, as if sleeping,
resting and waiting for the sun's expansion,
unfolding the flowers, awaking the forest,
giving life, or is this life, this breathing,
this expanding and contracting. What is life
but God's very own breath? Might there be
any difference between me, the earth
and God? This living plant, my very soul –
life itself, unfolding and spreading out while
being reduced in size and drawn together,
expanding and contracting – breathing,
being at one with God and the universe.
Then I think of global warming, mountaintop
removal, emphysema, and polar bears, all
taking my breath away.

Time is the presence of God in the world of space, and it is within time that we are able to sense the unity of all beings.

Abraham Joshua Heschel

A BREATHING SPELL

The tiny community of Sharon sits much in the middle of Bracken County, Kentucky amidst rolling hills cradling tobacco farms, and pastureland for milk cows and Black Angus cattle. The people here are farmers for the most part while all others remain completely dependent upon the farm industry made possible by this rich land. The people who live and work in this beautiful county are modest and hard working and carry a wonderful sense of humor which at times expresses itself in a personal manner leaving people somewhat embarrassed, yet never with any lasting scars, but only with fond memories. The Sharon Presbyterian Church is about the only landmark indicating that you are in the Sharon Community. The church is a brick building just off the road surrounded with cornfields and pastures.

The manse was a white frame house located across the road from the church and was more than adequate for my family and me when I visited on weekends as a student pastor. We always looked forward to the weekends when we could enjoy this rural life, giving us a wonderful break from the city of Louisville and the rigorous life I had as a full time student and Joy who worked full time as a Registered Nurse. The Sharon Church consisted of a small number of intimate people mostly who knew one another all their lives and finding it difficult, or perhaps awkward, for an outsider to come into the community. This was of no fault of the people who were most friendly and accepting but rather the nature of this small community. It is often said in most Kentucky counties that unless you were born there it was impossible to be fully accepted on the same level as the inborn families.

I was just starting my student pastor experience with the Sharon Church, still trying to find my way and remaining nervous with preaching on a regular basis. On this particular Sunday morning after church I found a small group of men in the front yard of the church seemingly to enjoy fellowship with one another. I recognized one of the men as Harry whom I had met the previous Sunday. Harry had introduced himself as the new County Agricultural Agent and was visiting the church as a newcomer to the community. Of course I was eager to make an impression with the hope that he might join the church. Just as I approached the group I heard one of the men say, "Well Harry, you say you don't like the new preacher?" Then to add insult to injury this statement was followed up with, "Well, I didn't think you would admit it in front of him". I don't know who was the most embarrassed, Harry or me, even though the laughter from the group was a relief indicating that it was just a joke. We all soon saw this to be a type of bonding experience and not in any way to reflect anything bad or negative toward Harry or myself. Why has such a story, such a moment, remained with me all these years? Why would such playfulness in the front yard of a country church have such significance for me and allow such an event to be filed in my mind as important, perhaps even holy?

I will never forget the almost godlike appearance of Abraham Heschel, wearing a long full beard while drawing from an enormous unlit cigar, who engaged with students at Louisville Presbyterian Theological Seminary, and continues to give me partial answers.

The higher goal of spiritual living is not to amass a wealth of information, but to face sacred moments. In a religion experience, for example, it is not a thing that imposes its spiritual presence. What is retained in the soul is the moment of insight rather than the place where the act came to pass. A moment of insight is a fortune, transporting us beyond the confines of measured time. Spiritual life begins to decay when we fail to sense the grandeur of what is eternal in time. 1

For Abraham Heschel the Sabbath is not a place or space but rather time in which we celebrate life, enjoying one another and giving praise to God. "Call the Sabbath a delight: a delight to the soul and a delight to the body". 2 Sabbath creates an atmosphere for play and rest, for joy and holiness – a time to be fully human after having inhaled the divine that animates us and gives us life. The above story about the men in the churchyard is an example of Sabbath as playfulness – a time of joy, laughter and bonding. Most likely we are no more conscious of this spiritual presence than we are of our breathing – the very gift of life until we become mindful of it as,

> "...the invisible icon of the Divine. In breath-centered meditation, one rests the mind in the breath, returning again and again to the breath as the mind wanders. It is the breath that draws one back to awareness, to awakeness, to presence. In Christian meditation, it is the breath that draws one again and again to the awareness of God. To speak of our human breath as an icon means that it is both a reminder of God's presence and a window through which we may be drawn toward God's presence at any place, for the breath is the most portable icon. 3

To recognize what is *eternal in time* (Sabbath), and experience our breathing as the *invisible icon of the Divine,* is to sit in the very presence of God. Dianna Eck reminds us, "There is something sacred about that which enlivens us, breath in us".4 Heschel shows us how Sabbath gives life in laughter, stillness, peace, rest and harmony through sacred stories and experiences, staging an atmosphere for God's presence in time. Sabbath and breath is all about sacred life that God breathed into Adam (Gen. 2:7), which the Quakers call "that of God in us." The Hebrew word for this life is *ruach* the author of the animating dynamic of the created order.

As I sit and breathe I also remember another story that took place with the Sharon Community. My breathing becomes an *invisible icon of the Di*vine while my memory centers on the *eternal in time*. As I breathe I become mindful of the atmosphere and the awareness of being *within* the Sabbath, absent of space and things and livened to the very presence of God. I can recall this moment through that special invisible icon – the gift of life, *ruach* that animates and places me within Sabbath filled with rest and laughter.

Ralph Harrison was a hard working farmer who never failed to attend worship services with his family consisting of his wife and three daughters. They always sat in the same place on the same pew close to the pulpit. Ralph's index finger on his right hand was cut off at the second joint leaving a stump, which wasn't at all noticeable until he went to sleep just about the time I would begin my sermon. It seemed all so natural for Ralph to rest the side of his face against his right hand with that stump of a finger on the bottom of his nostril so that he appeared to be sleeping with his finger up his nose. I had a fellow student preach for me one Sunday and on Monday morning I asked him how everything went at the Sharon Church. He responded that all went well and he enjoyed being in the Sharon Community but wondered who that was that went to sleep with his finger up his nose.

This is a wonderful example of Sabbath in that Ralph had found rest, peace and comfort. It is not unlike many stories and experiences we have within time in which we recall the very presence of God – breathing spells in which we focus on the divine breath of life. Times that bring laughter, rest and joy, but also opportunity to mend our broken lives by sitting a spell knowing we are of Divine breath and *within* Sabbath which is a delight to the soul. The juxtaposition of breath and Sabbath are also healing, a spiritual resource when one is experiencing adversity or calamitous events in which there is little to no control.

Back in the 80's I was involved in a community referred to as *The White Train Vigil* with active members spread from Texas to Charleston, South Carolina. The White Train carried nuclear weaponry from a plant in Texas to U.S. Navy vessels in Charleston by route of Savannah, Georgia where I was living at the time. *The White Train Vigil* was a group of committed individuals who were willing to be called upon to protest nuclear weaponry and this rail transportation through neighborhoods. A group of nuns organized this movement, which involved tracking the train and informing us of its arrival in our particular communities. We would go to the tracks armed only with our candles, prayers and songs while the train was armed with machine gun turrets and armed guards. I found that this particular time and my breathing and the breathing of those around me was assurance of God's presence in that God was both in us and around us providing peace and serenity in a frightening and difficult time. I also found grief to be called for in that we were witnessing the manufacturing and transporting of weapons designed for mass destruction, designed to take away the *ruach* of God, the breath of life and the one thing that gives meaning and purpose for living. In these days of global warming we need also to be in deep grief for the mountaintops and streams that the mining of coal is destroying in Appalachia and the carbon footprints it is leaving all over the world. We need to be in grief for all the problems that we have caused the world for we all share the same *ruach,* animals, humans and nature alike. How can we overlook the war in Iraq and Afghanistan with the thousands of lives that have been taken? The sadness of this war leaves me in grief.

Behind my house is a field that I enjoy watching as it changes from season to season reminding me that we have a lot in common as my closing poem indicates. The field has a life of its own – it is born, as such, as it comes to life in the spring with green grass and then in the summer with various flowers blooming only to be cut for hay at which time it lays to rest. This field is alive with various critters and birds even when it is at rest. This field might not have breath and yet it has a divine window through which I am drawn back to awareness, to being more awake, to presence.

I contribute my sense of awareness and presence to my father who always demonstrated comfortableness within himself and around others. Dad was totally absorbed in the other, be it another person, a tree, or the open sky it always had his full attention. He had a sense of wonderment and exploration that would not leave him alone, a kind of intrigue or curiosity that stayed with him until, like a puzzle, solved.

Dad always talked of how nothing would be finer than to have a farm in Georgia. I have no idea where such thoughts originated but they were always apparent and verbalized as we traveled through the state of Georgia. On one occasion as the family was traveling through central Georgia my mother noticed the gas gauge had moved very close to the empty mark. Dad insisted we had enough gas and humorously remarked that if we were to run out of gas we would just goose it. It was not long until the car began to sputter and cough and then died on the side of the road. Dad jumped out and said he would get us some gas as he crossed the road, walked across a field disappearing from our sight. Mother was distraught not understanding why he would allow the car to run out of gas. My brother and I sat quietly in the back seat waiting for our father to return. It didn't seem long before we saw Dad coming back across the field with a woman walking beside him. They were talking and pointing and waving their arms and appeared to be enjoying themselves tremendously. When they got to the car Dad with much enthusiasm introduced the woman and said she and her husband own this big farm and grew corn, cotton, and had a large number of cattle, and on and on until mother interrupted him, asking, "But does she have any gas?" Dad responded, "Oh, yes, she is getting us some gas." His voice and mannerism said this as if it was secondary to the excitement he had found talking with this woman.

This story demonstrates Dad's need and desire to explore and wonder but most important his desire to meet people. Nothing excited Dad more than to talk with people, to listen to their stories, to know of their experiences, hardships and joys and to explore where they came from, how they got to where they are and what most excites them about life. Yet, I saw another side of my Dad. He could be at peace within himself in almost a meditative state. He would sit for hours and watch the birds and look at the trees and anything that might take to his liking. Then he would come up with questions. "I wonder how old those big tall elms might be?" "Where do you think all those people in their cars are going?" There is something spiritual about being able to sit still, to listen, watch and contemplate in a busy, noisy world. I have come to increasingly appreciate these characteristics and accept them as a gift from my father as I find myself having many of these traits.

In the evening of life I have found myself becoming more mindful of a divine presence, more than ever before, while becoming less interested in formal religion. I have been through some difficult times, which have left me physically, emotionally, spiritually and socially crippled. I contribute my recovery, and recovering, to the Sabbath as described by Abraham Heschel as a spiritual moment in time, realized only as I allow myself to take a breathing spell, remembering spiritual moments as 'invisible icons of the Divine.' These spiritual moments, eternal in time, have been and continue to be my wife, who has never given up on me, as well as my extended family, children and grandchildren, who continue to be with me even and especially in embarrassing times. I am also fortunate to be a part of a most loving and accepting faith community, providing love and support, a living presence in the midst of disparity; a community which lives out the teachings that Jesus so clearly preached on the mount that we know so well as the Beatitudes. I have come to appreciate the presence of those who are not afraid to take the journey with me; those who are able to sit a spell with me, to share a breathing spell and allow our very presence to take its healing course. Parker J. Palmer, founder of *The Center for Courage and Renewal,* said it so well while being interviewed by Bill Moyers.

> A new habit of the heart would allow us to take the brokenhearted experience in a new direction, not toward shattering into a million pieces but larger, more capacious, more open to hold both the suffering and pain of the world.... 5

We need to take a breathing spell from trying to control the world by force. Nine eleven is a perfect example with folk around the world stating, "we are all Americans," being empathetic with our loss and joining us in our grief. What an opportunity to connect and reconnect with our global neighbors examining the world situation and ways in which we could collectively respond more appropriately! The Scriptures (1 John 14:18) tell us that love casts out fear, if so, does fear cast out love? Fear seems to be the weapon of choice in the living of these days leaving us so often with the inability to love or to accept love in difficult situations. When fear casts out love we make irrational decisions only to compound our situation making it more difficult to resolve. Sitting a spell allows us time and space to take a deep breath, listen and engage with others allowing love to cast out fear. I seriously doubt if this can be done outside of a loving community that reminds us of bigger issues than ourselves. This is especially true with the health care issue that President Obama is trying so hard to pass through Congress. There was so much excitement, passion even, during the campaign for Obama's health care reform. The cries of 'Yes we can' have become 'I wonder if we can' all because of the well organized hate opposition. Deliberate lies and distortion of what Obama is trying to accomplish has set the health reform movement into a totally negative tailspin. Hate that goes so far as to depict Obama as a Nazi with posters showing him with a Hitler mustache, town meetings with no willingness to discuss the issues but only an over zealous crowd with hate toward Obama and others who are trying to see that all Americans have health care coverage. Such hate appears to be motivated by fear and insecurity, a fear based totally on "me"; what I need, what I might not get, what might be changed that will take away from what security I presently have. They need to get their 'me ' out of the way to experience a transformation that cares about all the people and not just about themselves. And shame on us who allow such fear tactics to cast out this love and care for all people. We should be bold enough to risk taking a stand for what is right and good for all of us rather than for just the few. Perhaps W.E.B. DuBois said it well, "The most important thing to remember is this: To be ready at any moment to give up what you are for what you might become."

Pema Chodron tells us, "Fear is a natural reaction to moving closer to the truth". Before leaving this chapter I quote Chodron on this important subject of fear.

> No one ever tells us to stop running away from fear. We are very rarely told to move closer, to just be there, to become familiar with fear. I once asked the Zen master Kobun Chino Roshi how he related with fear, and he said, "I agree. I agree." But the advice we usually get is to sweeten it up, smooth it over, take a pill, or distract ourselves, but by all means make it go away.

> We don't need that kind of encouragement, because dissociating from fear is what we do naturally. We habitually spin off and freak out when there's even the merest hint of fear. We feel it coming and we check out. It's good to know we do that – not as a way to beat ourselves up, but as a way to develop unconditional compassion. The most heartbreaking thing of all is how we cheat ourselves of the present moment. 6

A SEASONED LIFE

In the fall of life
a field lies cut and gray
alive in a dormant rest
cut by the powered knife.

Life continues to thrive
deep in the dead mat
covering a sleeping earth
where field mice abide

Hard winter winds blow as
snow increases the blanket cover.
Life secure in the deep
showing only a barren land.

After such a rest
green shows itself so slowly
as warm days evolve –
spring emerges at its best.

How well the body rejuvenates
after a well deserved rest,
even to bloom again
showing not the least regret.

Summer heat with humidity
thickens the field with color –
stamina in broad shoulders
but not without humility.

At the peak of life
the powered knife returns
beauty cut and scattered
and once again we lay at rest.

Epilogue

I suspect everyone has someone with whom they identify and with whom they feel has greatly influenced their lives. If not, then what a shame! How does one get through life without a strong identity with a particular person or culture or geographical area to which they can point that has helped to mold them into the person that they have become. Too often a person or a given arena of life has a negative connotation that has shaped them into an evil profile, acted out in devious or even criminal behavior. Do we put too much emphasis on persons or groups, disallowing our own inner strength or will power to shape us into the person that we become? I personally feel that my father has influenced me in various ways – many ways that I cannot even identify but just know that it happened.

I have talked with individuals who feel they have been forced to take a particular path. Sometimes parents are determined that their children go to a particular college and take up a profession of their choosing rather than to encourage their child to determine his or her own destination. When I share with others that my father always encouraged me to do what I wanted to do, they often tell me I am lucky. To have your parents give you not only the permission but also the encouragement to be your own person is one of the greatest gifts I can imagine. Too often children feel the pressure from parents and friends to be *successful,* meaning they ought to get into a profession in which they can make much money. Money was never a motivating influence with my father; he taught me to fully enjoy whatever type of work I chose.

I have come to believe that it is an attitude of *sitting a spell* that has greatly influenced me. Today such an attitude would be considered lazy and a waste. Most important is the surprise element that becomes possible when one allows time and space to have their way. True meditation is to get out of the way, allowing time and space to take over your life. This is difficult in a culture that programs and plans almost every moment of our lives. It is also difficult when we have prerequisites or dogma that always has to be factored into our lives. Now that I am retired and need not live up to any outside expectations or pressure, I find that I am more free to being open to the spiritual presence that is always making itself available if I can only be still enough to experience it. Previously my plans or the expectations of others most always got in the way. There is such a need to be successful or to make a difference and especially to be productive in some kind of material manner.

Working in the church I found this to be especially true. Within the church it is difficult to promote the concept of *sitting a spell,* allowing the spirit of God to have its way. Within the main line denominations this concept is even frightening; someone might say something or have a revelation that is not accepted within the religious community, making everyone uncomfortable. When we do allow others and ourselves *to sit a spell* amazing things begin to happen. Stories come to mind that we want to share, 'out of the blue' ideas emerge that surprise us and add so much to the overall family or community in which we are a part. In a counseling relationship I have found that counselees often appreciate silence – a time to *sit a spell.* Sometimes such moments will bring unexpected tears and at other times laughter that was long over due, not being allowed because of the pressure and/or expectations of others.

I had a poet once tell me that poetry should always have a purpose, a plan and that the writer should always know what he or she is writing about. I totally disagree with this idea having written poetry myself. What is most important in writing poetry is time and space, a place to be and a space that allows for inspiration. Time is important in that one should not feel any pressures but rather allow the time to

212

have no particular beginning or ending. Time and space never fail me and always surprise me. When I am still and remain open something always comes that allows me to write poetry. I have yet to understand this, for it is beyond understanding and can only be experienced. I am increasingly convinced that God's presence and message come from the unconscious. It is when we are least expecting God's presence that it comes to us. We need only remain open to such possibilities and embrace it fully as a divine gift. We are not in control of such moments nor can we make them happen. We can only make room for them to happen. We often talk about our gifts and yet the greatest gift of all is God's gift to us that comes in many surprising ways. Perhaps we work so hard on finding and developing our personal gifts or talents that we fail to experience the greatest gift of all – the very presence of God that keeps coming to us if we can only be still, listen and wait. Advent is not seasonal but rather a year round experience that invites us to Come Sit a Spell.

I was recently in a doctor's office waiting for my appointment. I was enjoying the Classical music that was quietly playing. I then over heard a women speak to another woman, saying, "If I had to listen to that music for very long I would go crazy." I suspect her statement was not just about her music preference but rather her sense of being uncomfortable in such a low stress setting. In that waiting room was just the lovely music and us. We all need a certain amount of stress but perhaps we have way too much stress in our lives when we have difficulty sitting a spell.

The statement of 'come sit a spell' has always intrigued me. I married into a rural Appalachian family that lived on a small farm in Lawrence County. I often heard my mother-in-law use this phrase when people dropped by for a visit: 'Don't be in any hurry now. Come on in a sit a spell.' While a pastor in two small churches in Lee Country I often heard this phrase when I would pay a visit to my parishioners.

I have heard some people say that this was just a custom and that folk did not really mean it when they said, "come sit a spell". But it appears to me the people who feel this way are not from Appalachia.

This phrase has different meaning according to the context in which it is used. It always refers to a short, indefinite period of time. Sometimes it is used as one's turn at work. "I reckon I could dig in that hole for a spell." Or, it might be used for a period of work. "I've got to go work for a spell now." The dictionary tells us that Australians use this phrase for a period of rest. I suspect this is a carry over from England.

I have taken the liberty in using this phrase of 'come sit a spell' in a broad context as my book has indicated. I feel it is a rich phrase that has many applications within our families, the work place and community at large.

APPALACHIAN MORNING

Gladsome hearts listen to the silence as
tortoise moves slowly on paved drive,
unconscious of any danger
yet secure within its shell,
while birds frolic in early morn chatter
all for the better in this Appalachian valley
awaiting a new day, lying
mysteriously in foggy hollows.

Gladsome hearts listen to the silence as
morning awakens slowly this November day
with a slight damp chill as
souls anticipate the warm sun.
Chickadee sings, *Sweet-sweet*
while doves pair and coo in silence,
a non-anxious presence for an embracing couple
joyfully watching creation in the making.

Gladsome hearts listen to the silence
far from commuter trains and airplanes
replaced with donkey's braying
while horses nibble on green pasture
far from Chicago's rush,
more like a brush of an angel's wing
in the whisper of this morning
the making of a new day.

Questions for Pondering

Chapter 1: Beginnings

1. What are some of the early icons of your life? Spiritual windows by which you see most clearly, that which has molded and shaped who you are?

2. How might the opening poem of this chapter apply to your life?

   > roads run backwards
   >
   > as well as forward
   >
   > dreams and memories merge.

3. When you are working to accomplish a task what's most important, the journey or the finished task?

4. What might be some of the heartstrings that are tugging at your soul?

Chapter 2: Street Preacher

1. What keeps you from embracing or romancing your dark side?

2. Have you ever been shamed, misunderstood and/or avoided for turning aside to listen to the voice within?

3. Where do you find the "holy" or "spiritual strength" that empowers you to serve effectively in an indifferent world?

4. How might the poems speak to you in the living of these days?

5. How might the "holy fool" or "fool for Christ" concept be applied in this age of logic, data and reason?

6. Ever felt you were on holy ground? Recall the experience and share it with someone you trust.

Chapter 3: Back Again

1. How do you handle your sense of being wounded?

2. A psychiatrist once said, "If you have someone who will listen to you, you best beat a path to his/her door." Do you agree or disagree and why?

3. Who allows you to be blue?

4. Where do you experience healing in community?

5. How do you interpret the poem that opened this chapter?

> ice covers deep scars
>
> allowing only beauty
>
> of this Appalachian trail

Chapter 4: Candy

1. C.G. Jung states that the number four represents wholeness, not three, as Christianity has traditionally proclaimed in the trinity. Does the trinity represent too much goodness or brightness? Would this divine representation not be more complete if evil were not represented? Can the inferior compliment the perfect? Can it be possible that the rejection inferiority or darkness of Candy bring wholeness to all four – Candy and the three daughters?

2. How do you understand the concept of "home" within a psychological and spiritual sense? When do we know we are "at home"? Are we ever fully at home in the sense of being comfortable with God, others and ourselves? Or is there a difference between these three?

3. Does Wanda represent a positive concept of "home" – a comfortable community no matter what the circumstances? How do our families, home or community become sick and therefore not a good place to "hide" or call "home"?

4. How do you feel about the church that quickly condemned Candy once she got pregnant? Do you think her baby should have been baptized under these circumstances?

5. How do you think the church might be more helpful in strengthening our marriage and family life?

6. Do you see marriage and family life as a deeply spiritual gift that should be held accountable to God? How might this take place? What does this have to do with "being at home"?

7. How might these reflections on marriage and family life apply to our larger communities such as the neighborhood, town or city, state, nation and world at large? Are we living in good faith as a nation among nations or are we more like the rich man and Lazarus?

Chapter 5: The Purple Duster

1. What personal and spiritual value do you place on this concept of "falling upward" rather than the more traditional concept of "original sin" or "the fall from grace"?

2. John A. Sanford understands myth as an icon or "...pictorial representation of what is taking place in the Soul." Does this concept of myth add or take away from your own spiritual journey?

3. Within your own spiritual/psychological journey how do you experience breaking out of the garden?

4. Why would God place a serpent in the garden? Are perhaps the Gnostics correct when they refer to the serpent as "...the spiritual redeemer of man and God as the evil demiurge'?

5. Is the garden still alive and well today? What kind of box does the church or society place us in today? Do we just go along with the traditional belief? What happens if we try to get out of the box? What happens if we stay in the box? See movie *Mona Lisa Smile*.

Chapter 6: The Commune

1. Community, commune, communication and communion – is it possible to have one without the other?

2. What does it mean for you to think out of the box?

3. What kind of stories do you have within the context of sacred spaces?

4. Does the institutional church make possible sacred spaces?

5. How do you understand or experience God's play within community?

6. Discuss with another the poem that introduced this chapter. What do these words mean to you – "profane or holy all look the same"?

Chapter 7: Go Slow

1. Are people where they need to be regardless of our need to change them?

2. Might God be using the agnostic in a manner that is not possible through the people of deep faith?

3. How might people of Metropolitan America benefit

from a missionary visit from Appalachian people? How is the Metropolitan America wounded, and in need of healing?

4. What is spiritual about "sitting a spell"?

5. Give some examples of how your life and/or the lives of others are maxed out and in need of margins. How might structuring time to do nothing be beneficial?

6. Give examples of how "embracing the moment" differs from our normal racing through life.

7. How much is enough? How might enough be measured?

Chapter 8: Eat Half As Much, Chew Twice As Long:

1. Has commercialism created a society of neurotics manifested in obesity, substance abuse, and various kinds of violence including war?

2. How have families changed most in this age of commercialism that demands such a fast life style?

3. Is our fast complicated lifestyle based on fear? If so, how? What do we fear most?

4. Does listening and waiting just create more anxiety?

5. Does the institutional church help us to slow down and be less anxious or add to the problem?

6. What are the spiritual issues for you in this chapter?

7. Was the word of the Lord rare in Samuel's day because no one was listening? What about today? Do you expect to hear your name?

Chapter 9: Nine Eleven

1. What does it mean to be hungry yet eating in all the wrong places?

2. Why do you think America all but ignores poor countries and invests so much in wealthy countries?

3. Discuss with others this idea that America is in deep denial. What does this have to do with nine eleven?

4. Do you feel nine eleven was a catalyst to help us work out of our complacency?

5. Discuss the idea of James Hillman that it is the American habit of belief that appeals to our main mediocrities.

Chapter 10: The Full Essence Of Life

1. What distinction, if any, do you make between written prayers, verbal prayers and living prayers?

2. Are some prayers hollow? How so?

3. Is the *Lord's Prayer* intended to be a spoken prayer or a living prayer?

4. Do you think prayer makes any real difference in our lives? How so?

5. What part of the opening poem speaks most to you? Discuss with others.

6. Do you think we pray with any real understanding of what God wishes for us as His created people?

7. In a world that is so polarized how do you understand the story about the Rabbi's son?

Chapter 11: A Breathing Spell

1. What connection do you make between breath, air, wind and life?

2. What does it mean to be fully present with eternal time?

3. Do you agree or disagree that we ought to be in grief for the earth? Explain your answer.

4. What does it mean to you to "take a breathing spell"?

5. Dianna Eck describes breathing as an *invisible icon of the Divine*. Do you agree or disagree? Explain your position.

Credits

Chapter 1: Beginnings

1. Jones, Loyal, *Appalachian Values*, Berea College Appalachian Center, Berea, Ky. (Reprinted from Voices from the Hills, Robert J. Higgs and Ambrose N. Manning (eds.). New York: Edward Unger Publishing Co., 1975.

2. Buber, Martin, *I and Thou*, Second edition, 1958, Charles Scribner's Sons, New York, pp. 26, 27.

3. Kopp, Sheldon B., *If You Meet the Buddha on the Road, Kill Him*, Mass Market Paperback, 1988.

Chapter 2: Street Preacher

1. Blessed Xenia – Fool for Christ of Saint Petersburg, may be found on the Internet under, *Fool for Christ*.

2. The Jerusalem Bible

3. Connie Zweig, PhD and Steve Wolf, PhD, *Romancing the Shadow, Illuminating the Dark Side of The Soul*, Ballantine Books, New York, 1997.

4. Kelsey, Morton, *The Other Side of Silence,* Paulist Press. New York, 1995, p. 212

5. Ibid, p. 129.

Chapter 3: Back Again

1. Perera, Sylvia Brinton, *Queen Maeve and Her Lovers, A Celtic Archetype of Ecstasy, Addiction, and Healing,* Cattowmore Books, New York, 1999, pp 56 and 58.

2. Kidd, Sue Monk, *When The Heart Waits, Spiritual Direction for Life's Sacred Questions*, Harper and Row, San Francisco, 1990, pp 47,48.

3. *Who's Got the Blues?* By David Hajdu, Mother Jones, September + October 2003.

4. Chodron, Pema, *When Things Fall Apart*, Shambhala, Boston, 2005, pp. 108-109.

Chapter 4: Candy

1. Neumann, Erich, *Amor and Psyche, The Psychic Development of the Feminine*, Commentary on the Tale by Apuleius, Princeton University Press, 1956.

2. Nouwen, Henri J.M., *The Return of The Prodigal Son – A Story of Homecoming*, Image book – Doubleday, New York.

3. Sanford, John A., *The Kingdom Within, The Inner Meaning of Jesus' Sayings*, Harper, SanFrancisco, 1987, p. 140.

4. Ibid, p. 141.

Chapter 5: The Purple Duster

1. Edinger, Edward F., *The Bible and the Psyche, Individuation Symbolism in the Old Testament*, Inter City Books, Toronto, 1986, p. 20.

2. Sanford, John A., *The Man Who Wrestled With God*, Paulist Press, New York, 1987, p. 104.

3. Jung, C.G., *Answer to Job*, Bollinger Series, Princeton University Press, Princeton, New Jersey, 1996, p.16.

4. Jung, C.G., *Jung on Evil*, Selected and introduced by Murray Stein, Princeton University Press, Princeton, New Jersey, 1996, p. 129.

5. Jung, C.G., *Memories, Dreams, Reflections,* Vintage Books, New York, 1963, p. 43.

6. Fox, Matthew, *Sin of the Spirit, Blessings of the Flesh, Lessons for Transforming Evil in Soul and Society,* Three Rivers Press, New York, 1999, p. 2.

7. *Mona Lisa Smiles,* film directed by Mike Newell and starring Julia Roberts, December, 2003. (For further discussion on "falling upward" or becoming fully human in a world that wants to keep us in a box. Women especially might find this movie of special interest.)

8. Keen, Sam, *Hymns to an Unknown God,* Bantam Books, New York, 1994.

9. Sanford, John A., Ibid, p. 107.

Chapter 6: The Commune

1. Kornfeld, Margaret, *Cultivating Wholeness, A Guide to Care and Counseling in Faith Communities,* Continuim, New York, 1998, page 21.

2. Harrison, Steven, *Doing Nothing, Coming to the End of the Spiritual Search,* Jeremy P. Tarcher/Putham a member of Penguin Putnam Inc., New York, 1997, opening dedication page.

3. Ibid, Jones, Loyal, p. 5.

4. Ibid, Harrison, Steven, p. 79

5. Grant, Brian, *A Theology for Pastoral Psychotherapy, God's Play in Sacred Spaces,* The Harworth Pastoral Press, New York, 2001, p. 16.

6. Ibid, p. 13.

7. Tolle, Eckhart, *A New Earth, Awakening to Your Life's Purpose,* Plume, 2005, p. 108.

8. Ibid, p. 109.

Chapter 7: Go Slow

1. Swenson, Richard A., M.D., *Margin, Restoring Emotional, Physical, Financial, and Time Reserves, to Overload Lives,* Navpress, Colorado Springs, Colorado, 1992.

Chapter 8:
Eat Half As Much, Chew twice as Long

1. Pieper, Josef, *Leisure, the Basis of Culture,* Random House, Inc., New York, 1963, p. 58.

2. Ibid, p. 59.

Chapter 9: Nine Eleven

1. Sanford, John A., *Evil, The Shadow Side of Reality, Crossroad, New York, 1992, p. 58.*

2. Ibid, *p. 60.*

3. *Naipaul, V.S., A Turn in the South,* Vintage International, New York, p. 29.

4. Vivienne Pinto and Warren Roberts, Complete Poems of D.H. Lawrence. Viking Press, New York, 1954, p.522.

5. Fox, Matthew, *Sins of The Spirit, Blessings of The Flesh,* Three Rivers Press, New York, 1999, pp. 167-168.

6. Hillman, James, *The Soul's Code, In Search of Character and Calling,* Random House, New York, 1996, p. 268.

7. Ibid, p. 268.

8. Ibid, p. 269.

9. State Income Tax Burden on Low-Income Families,

Internet.

10. Ibid, James Hillman, p. 43.

11. Ibid, James Hillman, p.247.

Chapter 10: The Full Essence of Life

1. Foster, Richard J., *Prayer, Finding the Heart's True Home,* HarperSanFranciso, *1992, pages 217, 219.*

2. Armstrong, Karen, *The Battle for God, A History of Fundamentalism,* Ballantine Books, New York, 2000, p. 368.

3. Ibid, p. 368.

4. Harrison, Steven, *Doing Nothing, Coming to the End of the Spiritual Search,* Jeremy P. Teacher/Putnam, a member of Penguin Putnam Inc, New York, 1997, p. 60.

5. Merton, Thomas, *Contemplative Prayer,* Image Books DoubleDay, New York, 1990, p. 24.

6. Tolle, Eckhart, *A New Earth, Awakening to Your Life's Purpose,* A Plume book, 2006, p. 78.

Chapter 11: A Breathing Spell

1. Hesche, Abraham Joshua, *The Sabbath,* Farrar, Straus and Giroux, New York, 1983, paper, p.6.

2. Ibid, p.18.

3. Eck, Dianna L, *Encountering God, A Spiritual Journey from Bozeman to Banaras,* Beacon Press, Boston, 1993, paper, p.122

4. Ibid, p. 368.

5. *Finding Wholeness in Tough Times,* Bill Moyers Journal, PBS, February 20,2009.

6. Chodron, Pema, When Things Fall Apart, Shambhala, Boston, 2005, p. 5.

PHOTO CREDIT

Public Domain: FSA: *Destitute Pea-Picking Family in Depression* by Dorothea Lange, Original source National Archives and Records Administration.

"What We May be" Mary Southard, CSJ, Congregation of St Joseph of La Grange, Courtesy of www.marysouthardart.org

Public Domain Collection: Available through the Department of Defense, *World Trade Center Memorial* by Denise Gould.

Twin Tower view from Empire State Building 86th Floor Observatory. Three months before the September 11, 2001 attacks. Released to Public Domain by Germanramos.

CPSIA information can be obtained
at www.ICGtesting.com
Printed in the USA
FFHW011504061219
56475624-62357FF